Help! I've got a teenager!

Help!
I've got a
teenager!

ROBERT T. BAYARD, Ph.D.
& JEAN BAYARD, Ph.D.

EXLEY

First published in Great Britain 1984 by Exley Publications Ltd,.
16 Chalk Hill, Watford, Herts WD1 4BN.

© 1981 by Robert T. Bayard and Jean Bayard
© this British edition 1984 by Robert T. Bayard and
Jean Bayard

British Library Cataloguing in Publication Data

Bayard, Robert T.
Help! I've got teenagers!
1. Adolescence 2. Parent and child
I. Title II. Bayard, Jean

306.8 '74 HQ796

ISBN 1-85015-008-7

Reproduced, printed and bound in Great Britain by
Hazell Watson and Viney Limited, member of the BPCC
Group, Aylesbury Bucks.

For our beloved parents
Mary Bayard, Thomas Bayard, Elsa Holwerda, Gerhardus Holwerda

and children
Dona Sauerburger
David Bayard
Bernard Bayard
Thomas Bayard
Lynda Easley

Illustrations by David Lock

Appreciations

Contact with some remarkable persons has helped us in developing the ideas behind this book, and in making the book itself. We are grateful:

Especially to the many desperate parents and their teenage children who worked as clients with us.

To Pat Kaspar, our consulting editor.

To Catherine Young, Ph.D., Al Stratton, Ph.D., Helen Mehr, Ph.d., colleague, consultant, and friend, Arthur Bodin, Ph.D., and to Richard Fisch, M.D., Paul Watzlawick, Ph.D. and John Weakland, of the Brief Therapy Group, Mental Research Institute.

And to our colleagues of the Emergency Treatment Centre, Santa Clara:

Diana Everstine, Ph.D., Director
Ellen Bader, Ph.D.
Mike Barraza, M.S.
Ione Binford, M.S.
Carolyn Cameron, M.S.
Fred D'Aguinaga
Christine Dusek, M.S.
Louis Everstine, Ph.D.
Stephen Fields, Ph.D.
Edith Groner, M.S.W.
Harold Johnson, Ph.D.
Margaret Johnson
Novelle Johnson, M.S.
Ferol Larsen, M.A.
Jay Livingston, Ph.D.
Marcia Porter, Ph.D.
David Rasch, M.S.
Christine Remus, M.A.
Sheri Rosso
Edith Savage
David Fenstermarker, M.S.
Manoucher Tavokoli, Ph.D.
Richard Toft, Ph.D.
Judy Tombrink, M.S.
Matthew Turnbo, M.S.
Eileen Valcov, Ph.D.
Deak Van Arsdale, Ph.D.
Madelyn Witt, M.S.

Contents

Preface

If you are feeling worried or troubled about your teenager, we want to extend to you a welcome and to share with you, through this book, a way of easing your load. Do not feel alone, for there are thousands of other parents experiencing much the same problems you are, and the chances are that some of them are very close to you – near neighbours and friends. You may not realize you have this much company, because in our society the parent is 'supposed' to feel ashamed when a son or daughter shirks school or gets drunk or otherwise behaves foolishly, and therefore even friends tend not to confide in each other about how their children are really doing and how they, the parents, really feel about it. Your friends, to show a polite interest in you, may still greet you with the question 'How are the kids?' but the appropriate answer is to tell them about the socially-approved things your children are doing, not about the rebellions, the fights, the late nights, the truancies. To let the negative things become known would somehow mark you a failure as a parent, and the others you know feel the same way about it, so everyone keeps quiet and feels desperate in private.

We, Bob and Jean Bayard, have gone through this kind of experience, and so feel a special kind of interest in the situation of beleaguered parents. To us, it's vitally important which of two ways you go in resolving that situation. It will almost certainly look as if the problem originates in something your child is doing, and as if the solution lies in somehow changing your child, getting him or her to behave differently; however it will almost as certainly be better handled by seeing it as an opportunity for you to change something about your life, expanding it and learning to take better care of it. In this book we give you our ideas on how to take the second way, for the benefit of you *and* your youngsters.

We did not always feel so confident about how to handle these situations as we do now. We have brought up five children, and in the process we have done almost every one of the things, either wise or foolish, that we talk about in this book. The kinds of things our children did is their story to tell, and we respect their privacy, so we will say only that we have probably lived through as wide a gamut of teenage behaviour as any of the parents we have worked with, and our feelings about it coloured our lives for many years.

After bringing up our first two children nearly to adulthood, we seemed still to have plenty of fatherly-motherly feeling left. (Did we also want to prove we could be good parents and therefore worthwhile people?) At any rate, it was with joy and a sense of adventure that we adopted three more children, an eleven year old and two five year olds, from Korea. By the time all five were grown and ready to go out on their own, we had had thirty consecutive years of bringing up children.

Our experience during that period was one of ups and downs. There were times when the youngsters were 'doing fine' and then we felt fine, too. At other times they did the kind of things we talk about in this book, and then we felt unhappy – hurt, angry, and trapped. Every incident of this sort that came up touched off some basic, very uncomfortable feelings in the two of us. For Bob it was ideas like:

There is something wrong with me.

I can't establish a good, close relationship with my children.

They do not see me as a person.

For Jean it was a feeling of guilt and dread:

I must be a bad person.

I should be giving my whole life to the children. Instead, I am going to college or working part time. This is depriving them in some terrible way, and that's why they're misbehaving.

We were both ashamed of these feelings and suffered alone with them for a long time. Much later we came to see them as simply poor habits of thinking which we believe many parents in our society become caught in, and which can very well be changed.

To help with all the difficulty we were experiencing in child rearing we tried everything we could find that held out any hope for us.

We read books on caring for children. Some were very good; however most of them added to our guilt because they talked only about what parents could do for the child's sake, and we read into this the implication that our own lives should not matter.

We took the children to psychotherapy sessions for years. Probably this helped in some way, but the main result we *saw* was that our children came to believe they were 'patients', had something wrong with them, and needed help to get going on anything in life. We were so ashamed of having to resort to counselling that we never told any of our relatives or friends.

We took a class based on Dr. Thomas Gordon's Parent Effectiveness Training book. This was the first real help we experienced. It gave us a start at becoming equal members in our own family, and at seeing our teenagers as interesting and worthwhile responsible people.

We studied family life and psychotherapy at the university, and took advanced degrees in psychology.

We began working as professional counsellors for teenagers and their families who were in crisis. By now we have worked with hundreds and hundreds of vulnerable, rebellious, angry, sad, or determined teenagers and their (usually) desperate parents. Much of what we see in these situations seems familiar to us, and we feel that we understand it.

We have noticed in doing this crisis work that it is usually the parents who are worried when things seem to go wrong. Very occasionally a few teenagers ask us for help in getting off drugs or alcohol, for instance, but very, very few ask for help because they are associating with the wrong friends, lying, stealing, missing school, running away, etc. When children do these things, it is the parents who become desperate and call for help. That's why we're addressing this book to them.

We thought, worked, agonized, coped, over caring for our five. We had crescendos of weeping and high hopes, of despair and jubilation, of helplessness and triumph. All of these intensified as each child became a teenager and hit, as we experienced it, a peak

17

of being impossible to live with. We struggled earnestly through it all.

Eventually – and here is a note of beautiful hope we'd like to sound for every parent – the struggle began to ease. We began to notice, every once in a while, that we were actually at ease with our children, and about our children. Humour began to creep in; some of the things they said and did began to strike us as so human and so imbued with pathos that we understood them and had to smile even as we shook our heads and worried. Positive things that pleasantly surprised us began to happen more and more often; our children let us know, in meaningful ways, that they loved us, and every one of them did good and noble things of the sort that parents feel proud about. We found ourselves feeling utterly content with our children.

For a while we thought that this came about because they were finally maturing. Of course, they were but it's only lately that we have realized that we have changed. Our children were always loyal and sneaky, kind and inconsiderate, caring and selfish. Of course they matured, they changed in many ways, but as far as our relationship to them goes, we started out wanting something of them – that they turn out a certain way – and they have served as our patient teachers, doing the exact things that were needed to wean us from those expectations and free us to be able to enjoy them as they are. We feel a considerable debt to the experience we've had together. Without it, we might have gone all our lives with the same cosy but rigid expectations. They helped us enter a larger world.

That is the main contribution we feel we can make in this book – to encourage you, the parent, to see the present trouble with your teenager not so much as evidence of a bad or mistaken child but as a pressure upon you to expand and to change, and a chance to do so. Despite the pain, it's possible for you even to welcome this problem as one of the challenges, not of your child's, but of *your* life.

We can't of course pretend to have the 'answers' for a given situation, but we've had a lot of experience, we care about the happiness and responsibility of parents and children, and we can tell you what we'd be likely to try in your situation. We believe that the approach we describe, if you follow it, can make a large and happy change in your situation.

At times it will probably be difficult, even frightening.

It will require some changes in the way you think.

It may be exhilarating, too, and give you a sense of growth and liberation.

We suggest that you spend a couple of evenings reading through the book – the text, exercises, examples, and the rest – in a very relaxed way, just reading it through to let yourself get a general flavour of hope, ease, and a sense that things will be all right. Then start again at the beginning and work through each step in turn. We suggest working through the book in order because it would not be good to do the things at the end of the book without building up a background based on the earlier portion.

And – be kind to yourself. We can understand if you can't do some of the things we suggest, because we too were unable to do some of it in crises with our children. If we had it to do over again, knowing what we know now, we'd definitely follow our own advice, but we had to come through some hard learning and we made many mistakes. We forgive ourselves and hope you'll forgive yourself for whatever you can't do. Our hope is that you simply feel good about whatever things you can do, and that by reading this book you become a little more yourself and a little more able to change.

Chapter One

Getting the problem into perspective

This is a difficult time for you. You're upset, worried, maybe angry about something your teenager is doing.

It may be something private and very small in the eyes of the world:

> Jane doesn't seem to have any self-confidence. She spends most of her time in her room and at dinner-time she hardly talks to us.

It may be big enough for others in the community – school, police – to be involved in it.

> Dan's been stopped by the police for driving someone's car without a licence.

In any case it looms large for you and it makes you worried about how you son or daughter is turning out, what he or she will do next, and perhaps how you yourself will be able to stand living with this person until he or she reaches adulthood.

It may be any of the following things, all of which we've heard worried, caring parents complain about:

> Tom (14) steals money, drink, jewellery from us.

> Jan (13) stays out until all hours or even all night if she feels like it.

> He (17) won't do anything in the house. He's untidy every-

where – in his room, in the kitchen, and will not clear things up.

I know Linda (14) is on pot.

She (12) goes out with rough older friends who have nothing going for them and just hang around like scruffy dropouts.

Ann (16) has had two abortions. Now she's pregnant for the third time.

Mary (14) joined a Kung-fu club and as soon as I'd paid for the uniform, she decided to give up.

It's the lying I can't stand. I can't trust anything Karen (14) tells me to be the truth.

Martin (15) won't go to school; he hasn't gone for more than a few weeks in the last two years.

Cathryn (12) has been arrested for shoplifting.

It's the four-letter words. Dave (13) calls me names no boy ought even to say in front of his mother.

Emma (17) always wants to be by herself. She spends hours alone in her room.

He (16) won't be part of the family. He won't go anywhere with us and often he won't even talk to us.

She's had crazy hair styles for years. Now she's had part of her head shaved and she looks horrible.

My son (14) ran away; he's been at his friend's house for six days.

These things are naturally frightening to most parents, who take them to mean:

My son or daughter will turn out badly.

and

I have been a bad parent.

as well as, perhaps:

My child doesn't love me.

People will know I failed.

He or she has won, has beaten me.

I'm trapped to live like this with this person for another three (or five, or seven) years, and there's no way out.

Besides having these kinds of painful thoughts, you may be feeling extremely discouraged because it seems there is nothing you can do about the situation. You may have tried everything you could think of only to find that none of it helped for very long. You've tried to discipline him or her:

All right, you're not allowed out.

You did it again, so now you're not allowed out for the whole holiday!

Or you've tried 'rewards':

I'll give you five pounds if you don't miss any school this week.

I'll arrange an afternoon treat if you'll change your school uniform.

Or you've tried common sense parental guidance and orders:

'Anne, you should go to school and do your homework. If you don't, you won't be able to get a decent job later and you'll wish you had.

It's not right to steal, and you should not do it.

Don't treat your mother that way.

You may have tried direct supervision:

> I'm going to get you up at 7.00, drive you to school, escort you to your class, and pick you up straight after school.

You may have decided that perhaps your son or daughter needed understanding and love, and tried heart-to-heart talks and reassuring him or her that you care:

> Andy, why do you do these things? Let's talk about it.

> I love you.

You may have taken your teenager for professional help, only to find that things improved for a time and then deteriorated again, or even that things didn't improve at all or that your kid refused to go.

You may well have the feeling that you've tried every approach society has offered you and since none of them worked, there must be something lacking in you:

> What am I doing wrong? Where have I failed?

> I should have been here when you were little.

> Maybe it's because you have only one parent; I deprived you of your father (or mother) by getting divorced.

> And so on.

All of this makes for an extremely painful situation for a parent. It *hurts* to feel worried, helpless, humiliated, guilty. It is this pain we are tackling in this book. We want to tell you it may not be necessary for you to feel hurt in this way.

We believe that if you sincerely work on the approach we've outlined for you in this book, you can bring yourself into a happier situation, and at the same time do the most that is possible for you to do towards your teenager's best development.

As a matter of fact, there may even be positive aspects to the painful situation you're in at the moment. The worse the problem you're having with your teenager, the more likely you are to be badly upset, and therefore the more energy you may be willing to put into working on the problem and into changing. We will be

23

asking you to try some different ways of doing things, even of thinking, and it's often tempting to shrug off such suggestions. Your hurt and desperation may motivate you to try some of these new things and thereby be the cause of your finding a fuller and happier way of life for you and for your child.

Let's assume then that you're disturbed about something your teenager is doing and want a way of proceeding. We're going to describe such a way in five or six steps, with a chapter or two to cover each step. We suggest that you take each step seriously and spend some time on it before going on to the next one, for each step is based upon your having some mastery of all preceding steps. You might just browse quickly through the whole book first to get an idea of the total, but then we recommend settling down and working through each step in order. As we see it, you're in a painful situation which has taken a long time and a great deal of input from all family members to build up and it won't be resolved by throwing in a few superficial techniques. On the other hand, given an honest commitment on your part to work on it seriously and *persistently*, step by step, it seems reasonable that you should see some difference in the way things go within six to eight weeks. A sustained effort of several months would probably result in still further improvement.

Before we begin – a note on levels of parental participation. If you are a single parent, your effort alone will almost certainly yield positive results. If there are two parents involved in the upbringing of the child or children in question, it is a definite plus when both take the approach presented in this book. However if your partner declines to participate, it is still quite feasible for you to do it alone. In any case our experience shows that as long as any parent makes a sincere and sustained effort along the lines we are suggesting in this book, improvements will be achieved.

We are now ready to begin. The first step is to build confidence in yourself. We find that it is important, in working to improve the situation with your child, that you allow yourself to become encouraged about this possibility by relaxing, getting a perspective on your situation, and generally acquiring a degree of inner peacefulness. When you're feeling worried, upset, angry, you are likely to act impulsively and do things that actually get you the reverse of what you truly want. So now we ask you to spend a few minutes getting yourself into the proper mood for achieving something positive. You'll do best if you operate from a position of inner peace and relaxation.

You may have your own ways of doing this; perhaps you find

that walking a few miles or giving yourself a half hour to be alone without demands relaxes you and gives you a wider perspective. You may do some regular exercise that leaves you feeling fresh and relaxed. If so, we ask you to do this for yourself before you begin working through this book and to repeat it every time you find yourself in difficulties. In case you'd like to try some of our ways of building up your confidence, we're including here some exercises we find to be helpful. They may strike you as simple; don't let that blind you to the fact that if you give yourself to them, they can be very powerful. We find that only one factor really prevents a person from successfully feeling relaxed and self-confident about him or herself, and that is *failure to understand that it can be done.* Most people do not realize that they themselves make their own moods, and that therefore they can change them, and that it is all right for them to change them. If you give yourself permission, you can put yourself into a calm, everything-is-basically-all-right-and-now-let's-see-what-I-can-do-about-this-problem, mood. We've seen people do it, and we've done it ourselves, and therefore we think that most readers will have the ability to do it.

In order to prepare yourself then before going on to direct work with the teenager problem, try going through the following sequence:

First, while sitting in your chair, relax your muscles, all of them except the few needed to stay sitting and hold your book.

One of the strange habits most adults develop is that of tightening muscles when we get into uncomfortable or stressful situations. It's a strange habit because the tightened muscles do not help us to get out of the bad situation; instead they tend to lock us even more tightly into it. It's well worth learning exactly the reverse response: *relaxing* our muscles whenever discomfort or stress arises. Doing this puts us into a far better position to resolve and change the problem.

With practice you will be able to relax quite thoroughly in a second or two. However, if you think of it as something that only takes that much time we can almost guarantee you will see it as unimportant, maybe try it once or twice, and then drop it entirely. Therefore we ask you to do a more systematic relaxing now and to do it again and again in the coming days and weeks until it is second nature for you, every time you become aware of any problem arising, to let go all muscles that are unnecessarily tense. *Relaxing your muscles will make it almost impossible for the situation with your kid to go on as it has been, if only because you will not be able to respond in that situation as you have been doing. It's possible you can't even get angry or worry if you're thoroughly relaxed.* Relaxing your muscles can also be extremely valuable for your physical health.

Right now, then, as you're sitting in your chair, first *tense up* every muscle in your body at once, as tightly as you can, and hold the tenseness for ten seconds or so. Sit there as tensed and rigid as you can get. Then let it all go – let your body sag limply into your chair. Notice how this feels, how the next breath after you let go tends to be slow and deep, and how you can then feel the tension leaving, draining away.

Now, continuing to sit quietly in your chair, spend at least ten minutes deepening the relaxation by mentally going over every part of your body and letting it relax even more. As you do, let a feeling of inner peacefulness spread thoughout your body as you give each part permission to relax.

'Now my toes are relaxing (as you let them go even more limp). Now, the arches of my feet are relaxing. Now, the heels. Now, the ankles are letting go and relaxing. Now my calf and shin muscles are relaxing still more.'

Continue thus, slowly and gently, over your entire body, returning to specific areas as needed until you can feel a satisfying degree of relaxation throughout your body.

Now, gently continuing with any sense of relaxation you achieved, and using only the muscles you need to hold your book and read, go on to the next step.

Sitting quietly, imagine now that there is a little piece of you, at the very centre of your being, which is very, very calm and happy. Undisturbed by all the worries and the fears about the future, there it sits, utterly peaceful, strong and happy. It cannot be touched. Picture it in terms of some image if you wish – a flame, a jewel, or a secret lake, calm, smooth, and without a ripple. Imbue it with a profound peacefulness and joy, a stillness; realize it is safe and strong. There it is, deep inside you. Imagine you *are* this flame or this jewel or this lake, deep at the core of yourself.

Imagine that this secret centre is going to be there within you always, staying there, calm and still, through all the tasks and problems and worries you will go through and that if you wish, *you can learn to remember it is there.* It is a little core of inner peace, and many times, as you go through your day, you can remember it and mentally touch it. Knowing it is there you can feel strengthened and relaxed for the encounters with your child which are to come.

Now holding the feeling of relaxation and of an inner peace, begin gently to expand your view of the world so that the problem with your child shrinks to a manageable size within that view. If

26

you've been feeling worry or resentment or other painful emotions when you think of this problem you have probably come to see it within a limited framework – a framework which is simultaneously limiting your creativity in working out solutions to the problem. You'll have more space with a widened perspective.

While remaining very relaxed, then, sit comfortably in your chair and let your thoughts dwell on the problem with your son or daughter. Picture you and him or her in this worrying situation. When you have this well in mind, think of both of you and the home you live in, along with anyone else who lives with you, so that you're now thinking of yourself and your teenager and whoever else may live there, all in your home.

Now, add the immediate neighbourhood. Think of the land and the little group of buildings that make up your neighbourhood, and all the people there – you and your teenager and your neighbourhood and all the people in it. When this picture is clear in your mind, go still further and think of the whole county – you, your son or daughter, and all these other hundreds of parents and children and other people working and interacting and all this stretch of land. Enlarging it further, think of your whole country, millions of people and families, millions of acres of land, cities, fields. Having thought this far, now picture for yourself the whole earth, the land and the oceans and the people. Backing now much further away, let yourself think of the whole earth and all the rest of the solar system – a vast burning sun and massive planets, moons, cosmic dust wheeling slowly around it. Imagine now the entire galaxy – whole clusters of solar systems, stretching out so far you can get a grasp of the distances between them only by marvelling at them. Then let yourself imagine the universe – millions of galaxies spread out in all directions, to an end no human being has yet imagined.

Continuing to keep in mind the sense of this immensity of being, come back to think of the problem with your son or daughter, and assign it its proper importance in the scheme of things. Realize that yes, it is a real, tangible problem – and yes, in all this vastness of being, you can probably trust it to work itself out somehow, no matter what you do, without resulting in any real or lasting damage in our total world.

Now imagine that you are on a very relaxed holiday in Italy, and that you are browsing through the ruins of the ancient city of Pompeii. It is a calm, sunny day. As you look around, you see on all sides the evidence of the everyday life of the past – streets and rows of fallen houses, patios, kitchens, stone wine casks. Hundreds of years ago people worked, talked, cared for families, in this place which is now very still, basking in the warm sun. Imagine that in this quiet place you now come upon a stone column on which some householder of the ancient city recorded the events of his daily life, and you see written there: 'Today I was filled with dread and anger because my son was picked up by the Pompeii police' – or, 'Today I realized that my daughter is smoking pot.'

Notice how much or how little adrenalin you generate at the thought of that parent's dilemma in that long ago time. It may be that you experience a certain compassion and fellow feeling for him or her, but very little real anxiety.

Now imagine that you were that householder, that it is your problem with your child that is inscribed on the stone column, and that nearly 2,000 years have passed since it all happened. Notice how you feel about the problem in this light.

. . . .

Now, in your present, nicely relaxed frame of mind, continue reading and consider with us some important facts:

Most youngsters who do the kinds of things we listed at the beginning of this chapter turn out extremely well; that is to say, as adults, they manage to support themselves and pull their weight in the world while maintaining reasonably comfortable relationships with others in their lives, including their parents. The probability is that no matter how worried, angry, despairing you have been feeling about it, the situation will improve and your child will turn out to be a reasonably decent and happy person.

Most families go through a period during a son's or daughter's adolescence in which parents and children have trouble living together. Most teenagers, including the ones who do the things we've listed above, make a psychological return later — usually sometime between eighteen and twenty-five — and become friends with their parents.

You have lots of company. Thousands of parents are going through what you are, and thousands more have gone through it in the past and come out on the other side.

You probably have not ruined your child even if you're thinking with a great deal of guilt that you have been a 'bad parent'. There is a tremendous force in young people – as in people in general – which presses to fulfil their lives, and this force, more than anything you could do or not do, determines how they turn out. It is clear that there is a great range of different environments in which young people can grow up successfully – in Central American villages in which they're isolated in dark huts for their earliest years, in Eskimo igloos, in native tribes in which they're brought up by other children or the village adults in general and rarely see their parents.

If you're feeling trapped, resentful, and that your teenager has the upper hand, you almost certainly have more power than you think you have, including the power to change things so that you feel better. Doing this, far from being destructive to the kid, would probably be beneficial for both him or her and you.

Here is a final daring thought you might consider:

You have as much need for and right to happiness, freedom, consideration, love, and so on, as your teenager does.

We'll assume you're feeling ready now to begin working on the specific problem you're having with your teenager. First, let's look to see exactly what your goal is. What is it you're after in relation to your son or daughter? If you can clarify and keep in mind what you want as you interact with him or her, you can be more sure you're heading towards it and not simply digging yourself more deeply into the present stressed situation, which you don't want. What exactly is your goal?

Parents in this kind of situation are usually after several things at once, at different levels. At the most immediate, specific level, they want the kid to change the particular behaviour that is worrying them.

He can't go on stealing.

He's got to go to school.

I want her to come in on time.

I want her to stop using four letter words.

When asked to consider why they want these particular changes, parents are likely to respond with further goals at a somewhat more general level. For example,

I want him to stop stealing because:

I want him to be an honest person.

I don't want him to get into trouble.

He should go to school because:

I want him to go to university.

I want him to be able to get a good job.

She should come in on time because:

I don't want her to get into trouble in the big world.

Then, when they are asked what they are after in the most long-term way, why they're going through the many years of child-rearing, they describe very general goals.

I want him to turn out to be a good person.

I want her to be happy.

I want him to have good relationships with other people in his life.

If we summarize and bring to the highest level what most parents seem to be after, the following goal covers most of it:

I want my child to turn out to be a decent, responsible person, able to make good decisions for him or herself.

Now, we have noticed something interesting about the process of achieving goals in interpersonal situations like the one between you and your teenager. We find that it works best and gives you the greatest chance of attaining your goals at all levels if you forget about the lower level goals for the time being and direct your energies towards achieving the highest goal. In fact, you cannot attain many of the lower level goals by going after them directly, and attempts to do so tend to worsen rather than improve the situation. Trying to make your son or daughter stop stealing, or go to school, may only lead to increased stealing or truancy especially when, as is often the case, the kid gets attention by doing them. However, these same lower level goals frequently fall into place when you aim towards the higher goal. For this reason we ask you to set aside the more immediate concerns for the moment – your worry over the current crisis, the specific situation with the school or the stealing or the undesirable friends. Instead, take the long-term view in your dealings with your son or daughter. In deciding how to behave in interactions with your teenager, drop that urge to push him or her to shape up in the specific situation and instead, ask yourself, 'What can I do in this situation that would contribute to my child being more responsible and able to make his or her own decisions?'

Chapter Two

Giving your teenager responsibility for his/her own life

At this point we are going to introduce some ideas which, if you are having trouble with your child, may surprise you – may strike you as selfish, or immoral, or revolutionary. If this is your reaction, we ask you to withhold judgment on these ideas until you have read through the whole book and understand our viewpoint, because, even though they may take some getting used to, we find them to be both humane and effective.

If you are experiencing troubles with your son or daughter, it is extremely likely that you're doing one or both of two things.

1. Certainly you are failing to do a job which is rightfully yours: *Making your own life happy.*

2. Very probably you are taking over a job which is rightfully your son's or daughter's and not yours: *Running your teenager's life.*

The work in this book is aimed to help you change on both of these counts. Because it's easier, we are beginning, in this and the next three chapters, with the second item, coaching you on getting out of running the youngster's life. We'll go into much more detail, but now, as a beginning, to get you into a more comfortable situation while you're working on the total problem, we ask you to take the following steps.

Step One

Sit down with paper and pencil and make a list, as complete as you can, of all the things your child does that bother you.

Even if there is someone else working on this problem with you, do the list and everything else in the book on your own, as an individual. If two parents are working on the problem together, each should make a separate list, and they will probably turn out to have at least some different items.

This list will be the basis of your work in this book, and we hope to coach you to do something about every item.

Once you get underway, you may be able to list eight or ten or more items. Here are sample items other parents have listed:

Things Teenagers Do that Bother Parents

Stays up late.
Lies, e.g.:
> *Says she is going one place but goes somewhere else.*
> *Says he did his homework when he didn't.*
> *Says she didn't steal from my purse.*

Leaves a mess in the kitchen.
> *Puts the breadboard away with crumbs still on it.*

Leaves wet towels all over the bathroom.
Leaves dirty dishes in the living room.
Doesn't feed his pets.
Doesn't clean up her dog's mess.
Uses my clothes without asking.
Dresses like a tramp.
Uses too much make-up.
Gives my clothes (hair dryer, cosmetics) away to her friends.
He has long painted nails and wears make-up.
She has vulgar tattoos.
Sneaks out of the window at night.
Stays out late or even all night.
Leaves his bicycle outside to be stolen.
Leaves my tools outside to get rusty, or loses them.
Hogs the phone for hours.
Runs up large long distance phone bills without asking me.
Won't change clothes after school.
Has a bad belligerent attitude.
Has a sullen attitude.
Goes around with undesirable friends.
Has an older boy friend (or girl friend).
Watches too much TV.

Lies around all day just listening to the stereo or watching television.
Doesn't do his homework.
Won't wear school uniform.
Won't go to school.
Is failing in school.
Brings friends into the house while I'm gone.
Lets other teenagers in who steal from us.
Doesn't take baths.
Won't do chores.
Has tantrums and makes threats when he doesn't get his way.
Won't clean up her room. Leaves it in a mess.
Runs away.
Fights with brothers or sisters.
Says I don't love her.
Swears.
Calls me names.
Won't do things with the family.
Wants to be by herself most of the time.
Demands money.
Tells others that I mistreat her.
Steals from me or others in family (money, jewellery, coin collections, drink).
Smokes.
Spends hours in the pub and is under age.
Drinks beer with friends.
Smokes pot.
Has pot in his bedroom.
Is sexually active and even promiscuous.
Threatens bodily harm to me or others.
Got his girlfriend pregnant.
Had an abortion, and now is pregnant again.
Knocks holes in the plaster when angry.
He wears an earring and a Mohican haircut.
Won't try to get a job.
Spends all her pocket money then demands more.
Won't pay for her keep.
Drives his motorbike too fast and won't wear a crash helmet.
Drives his motorbike when he's been drinking.
Takes someone else's car and goes 'joyriding'.
Breaks into our neighbour's house and steals things.
Goes shoplifting.
Threatens to kill himself.
Rides in cars driven by irresponsible friends.
Is damaging my relationship with my partner.

This is a dismaying list to read. If you'd read it before deciding to have children it might have influenced you to change your mind. There's a positive aspect to reading it though: you probably don't have all the problems on the list! We still think each of these problems can be seen as an opportunity around which you can change your life for the better rather than merely as a painful hassle. Let's begin now to sort out and bring some kind of order to your list.

Step Two

When your list is made, go over it and pull out for a separate 'pile' all the things your son or daughter does which, although they may have consequences for his or her life, will not affect your future life. We will call this the 'kid's-life pile'.

Spend some time on this, thinking about each item as you go along. As you check over your list, you will probably find that some items clearly affect only your teenager and thus belong on the 'kid's-life pile'; others clearly have consequences for your life and so do not belong on this pile. Still others you may have to break up into several pieces to find a part that affects you and a part that doesn't.

If you really get stuck deciding whether an item should go on this pile, ask yourself whether you have any direct power over this situation or not. For example, if the cosmetics you lend your daughter tend not to come back, you could stop lending. However, if she is in the habit of smoking cigarettes while out of the house, there's no direct action you can take to change it. In the first instance you have some direct power over the situation; in the second you don't. We find that items which do not affect your life tend to be things you can't do anything about anyway. We think it's poor tactics to make your stand in an area in which you're helpless to start with, and so suggest that if you can, you put these items on the kid's-life pile. Reserve your strength for areas we'll deal with later in the book in which you do have some leverage.

Of course, the way you select these items will depend on your unique situation; only you can decide whether or not a given item belongs on this pile of things that do not affect your life. Nonetheless, we can go over the list of examples above and suggest items that, by and large, might reasonably go on this pile.

The following items are generally best put on the kid's-life pile, reserving the rather small portions of them that do affect you and also fall under your control:

● **Stays up late.**

Parents often worry about this item on the grounds that a young person needs his or her rest in order to be ready to get up on time and be fresh for school the next day. It's true that staying up late may have this kind of consequence *for your teenager's life* – bleary eyes and drowsiness the next day, perhaps – and this pretty clearly doesn't affect your life. Consider putting this on the kid's-life pile, then, and reserve such aspects as the following, which do affect your life:

Is grumpy the next day.

Prevents me from having privacy and/or a quiet time at night.

Demands I wake him or her next morning.

● **Watches too much TV.**

We can think of consequences for your youngster's life here, probably the same ones you have worried about. He or she is probably wasting time; posture and use of the eyes is probably not the best, and the kid is allowing his or her mind to be filled with trivia instead of learning to enjoy using it creatively. None of this affects your life, so this item is probably for the kid's-life pile, with possible reservations like these:

Prevents me from watching my own programmes.

Has the TV on so long and so loud that the noise bothers me.

● **Doesn't take baths.**

A horrible picture haunts parents whose children won't wash: You're walking down the street with your child thirty years from now, you neat and polished, he or she an unwashed, scruffy and hangdog adult. Everyone you know sees you together and thinks, 'Something is terribly wrong with this parent, to let his or her child grow up to be such a slob.'

Apart from such shame, your teenager's not-washing probably does not affect your life, although it does have consequences for the teenager, whose friends, teachers, relatives, etc., develop an opinion of him based on his state of cleanliness, and probably treat him accordingly. Consider putting this item on the kid's-life list and reserve aspects like this if they are a problem:

> She smells, a stale sweaty smell every time she moves.

> He gets the furniture dirty when he sits on it.

> When it's his turn to cook he doesn't wash his hands, and I have the feeling the food's dirty.

● **Fights with brothers and/or sisters.**

This is one of the most common and expected worries for many parents with more than one child, and it takes so many forms and occurs in so many different intensities that we are still being presented with new variations. Each time a new one comes up we tend to think, 'This situation really is an exception,' and begin to work on it in a different way. Over and over again we are brought back to seeing it in the way we describe in this book.

Your major concern when children fight may be for their safety; you're afraid one will seriously hurt the other. Clearly this would have grave consequences for both hurt and hurter. Even if the outcome is not this drastic, you may fear they are developing life attitudes through the fighting, one learning to be a bully, the other to be a victim. These are serious consequences – and they affect primarily the children's lives. We suggest that if the children involved are old enough to run and to tell tales, you put this item on the kid's-life pile, keeping out aspects that do affect you directly:

> I'm frightened by the possibility of real injury.

> They make so much commotion – and I can hear the screaming, noise of scuffling, banging furniture – while they're fighting.

> They are so noisy that the landlord threatened eviction.

● **Screams, has tantrums, when doesn't get his or her way.**

You don't like your son or daughter to be displeased or angry with you, and you don't like neighbours or anyone else to know that this exaggerated behaviour is going on. Yet, tantrums probably don't have real consequences for your life. For the teenager we've known the screaming fits to result in a sore throat and hoarseness, feelings of helplessness at not being able to get what he or she wanted in a more appropriate way, and, sometimes, the exhilaration that comes from exploding once in a while. Thus this is probably a kid's-life item.

Some children throw things when they're angry; it seems to us that whether this should go on the kid's-life pile or not depends on whose things get thrown or get hit by the missiles. If they're your things, it certainly affects your life. If they're his or hers, it seems to us the loss if they are broken is the kid's, not yours, and we'd put the item on the kid's-life pile.

Tantrums are not simple. They are usually in reaction to something you have done and that something could involve either a kid's-life item ('No, you can't go to Iain's until your homework is done') or a parent's-life item ('No, I won't let you take my car tonight'). Tantrums occur too when there is a history of your giving in to your kid. In effect you may have trained your teenager to have tantrums by occasionally rewarding them. Now you must retrain him or her. We'll show you how in later chapters.

An aspect of tantrums which might be appropriate for your own pile is the noise. One mother we worked with had a real medical problem with her eardrum. Thus, for tantrums, perhaps you would want to reserve the following:

The noise annoys or gives me a headache.

- **Doesn't take care of personal belongings.**
- **Leaves bicycle out where it can get rained on or stolen.**

Almost any adult who has worked to support him or herself feels uncomfortable at seeing valuable things mistreated, and when they're things you have worked to pay for, the discomfort can be acute. Seeing the things you provided being treated cavalierly, you begin to feel unappreciated too. You may develop anxious and resentful feelings about money, also. You've paid for something that is not being valued and you may feel you're going to have to go on paying for more things, that your money could just dissipate like water going down the drain.

To change the situation around and put yourself back in control of your own financial outlay, we recommend making a distinction between things that belong to your teenager and things that belong to you, and put the way your teenager takes care of his or her own things firmly on the kid's-life list. It's pretty clear that the loss of your daughter's bike, ruining or soiling of your son's school uniform, the giving away of your child's money, is going to affect his or her life, and not yours. At the same time, reserve aspects of this item that certainly do have consequences for you:

Expects me to replace lost or ruined or given-away things.

● **Leaves his or her room in a mess.**

This one can rankle some parents almost unbearably, especially mothers. Yet in most cases it affects mostly the youngster's life; it is your son or daughter who must live in a pig sty atmosphere, feel ashamed to invite friends in, be unable to find things in the general disorder, perhaps have to wear unwashed and rumpled clothes.

Parents sometimes feel that it is part of their job to train their children to be neat, and that an important element of that training is to insist on a neat bedroom. We'd like to convince you somehow that this is best made a kid's-life item. If you had a lodger who was paying to rent the room, would you be insisting that he or she keep it tidy? We think probably not; if a person is paying for the room it's really his or her territory. Of course, your son or daughter is not paying for the room but it seems reasonable that some part of the house be set aside as really his or her territory. Put the cleanliness of your teenager's room on the kid's-life pile if you can.

A messy room would seem to affect you only in ways like these:

Leaves door open so I can't avoid seeing the mess.

Makes us run out of cups by leaving them in his room.

Attracts ants and mice into the house by leaving smelly food scraps.

Leaves room messy while we're trying to sell the house and want to show it to prospective buyers.

● **Won't do things with the family.**
● **Wants to be by herself most of the time.**

Parents tend to feel hurt, unwanted, rejected, when teenagers decline to go on family outings and seem to prefer being with friends or alone with a stereo. We'll describe later some things you can do to increase the chances of your son or daughter wanting to go out with you, and here merely suggest that if you can, you put this one on the kid's-life pile. Try thinking of it this way: that you are an interesting, caring, fun person to be with, and if your teenager does not choose to be with you, it is his or her loss rather than yours. Aspects you might hold in reserve if they apply are:

Prevents me from going out by refusing to accompany me, because I know he will wreck the house, bring other people into the house, and so on, while I'm gone.

Notifies me she isn't coming too late for me to be able to cancel reservations or make other arrangements.

● **Goes with 'undesirable' friends. The sorts of friends who may fall into this category for you are friends who clearly have values different from yours, or who are much older or who have been in trouble with police or who are into sexual activities, drugs, truancy and so on.**

'To be allowed to pick my own friends' is probably the second most common and urgent thing the teenagers we have seen say they want. The first thing is 'more freedom' and even that often turns out to mean 'freedom to be with friends of my choice'. At the same time we know that good parents are often geared to feel responsible for the kinds of people their children associate with, and school authorities and counsellors sometimes reinforce this responsibility. We've heard a probation officer tell the parents, 'You're responsible for the people your child goes around with.' However, this is also an item over which you have no direct control and it doesn't affect your life directly.

In our view, this item is an especially good one for you to use to gain increased freedom for yourself and at the same time score points with your son or daughter. We think it belongs squarely on the kid's-life list. Keep out for further consideration aspects of this item that do affect you, such as:

Brings these 'undesirable' friends home against my wishes.

Allows these friends to steal from me.

Has these friends in the house when I'm out.

Demands that I perform services for these friends (driving them to discos, parties and so on).

● **Runs away.**

The first time a child runs away can be a truly agonizing time for the parent. You will probably experience a real pain and inner pressure – a pain that distracts you from thinking of anything else for some time, a pressure of continual worry, hurt, shame. As long as your son or daughter is away, you will see him or her in every young person you pass who looks anything like yours and feel a pang every time. Nonetheless, we cannot say that it is the child who is bringing about all this painful feeling. Rather, it is something we parents do to ourselves on the occasion of a runaway, partly because we believe we should be able to control all of our children's behaviour and this action of theirs uncontrolled by us jars that belief, and hurts.

In a typical runaway situation, both teenager and parent see it as something the teenager is doing to the parent or parents, usually to try to get something (attention if nothing else). To give it some drama and to justify a basically irrational action, they often portray their parents, to any willing ears they can find, as five-horned, web-footed monsters, and the parents are likely to learn of this somehow in the process of the runaway. All of this can make it difficult to put running away on the kid's-life pile. Nevertheless we believe that this is the most effective place for it.

If we look at the young person as an individual responsible for his or her own life in the world, we can view the running away not as something done to the parents but as something the adolescent does with his or her own life, which affects that life. To the teenager belong the dangers, the excitements, the freedom of being away, the knowledge that he or she is being unfair to you, the problem of falling behind at, or dropping out of school, the job of finding friends who will put him or her up, the discomforts of having to spend a few nights in church gardens, in railway stations, in the doorways of supermarkets and so on.

We recommend, then, that you put this item on the kid's-life pile. Keep back aspects of the runaway that could directly affect your life:

> Leaves me legally and financially responsible for damages he or she might incur. (However, this also holds when your child is not a runaway.)

> Leaves me not knowing whether to continue to provide a room, groceries, etc.

● **Rides in cars or on motorbikes with irresponsible friends.**
Here your main concern is for your son or daughter's safety. You're picturing him or her badly injured or perhaps somehow responsible for others being injured. Certainly this item could have tremendous consequences for the teenager's future life and it's also something you can do very little about. If you forbid it, your kid would have the ability to do it behind your back and you would have lost even that small bit of control over the problem.

Therefore, we think this item belongs on his or her life list. An aspect you may also be worried about and which would affect you directly is:

> Being injured and becoming incapacitated and a burden, whom I would have to support.

● **Drinks, smokes, uses pot or other drugs.**

These activities may be harmful to health as well as illegal, so they certainly have consequences for your child's life. Aspects that affect your life could be:

Coming home drunk or high on drugs or glue.

Keeping drugs in the house (this may make you liable for prosecution).

Police involvement which requires a parental court appearance.

● **Is sexually active.**

As long as your son's or daughter's sexual activity takes place away from where you are, it would seem to affect your life only in quite circumscribed ways, while it has many possible repercussions for him or her. Issues of self image, relationships with other persons, morality, love, possible pregnancy, and venereal disease all enter in and are certainly important decisions for the youngster. If pregnancy occurs, even the decision about whether to keep the baby, give it up for adoption, or have an abortion belongs to the young mother.

Aspects that do affect you are things like the following:

Having sex with a girl under 16.

Having sex in our house.

Expecting me to raise the baby, while she goes out to college or work.

- **Stays out late.**
- **Sneaks out the window at night.**

Again, your main concern here may be for your son or daughter's safety. You think of all the dangerous things that can happen late at night – muggings, rapes, and so on – and you want your child to be safe at home. Your son's or daughter's safety certainly is an important factor in his or her life, and affects your life mainly insofar as you worry about it. If you can do so, put this one on the kid's-life list and reserve any aspects of it that do have an effect on your life, such as:

> Disturbs my rest by coming in noisily or by waking me up late at night.

> Breaks windows and door locks coming in or out, and marks walls and furniture by clambering over them.

> Leaves house open to possible break-in by leaving it unlocked.

- **Drives a friend's car without a licence (or steals a car and goes joyriding).**
- **Breaks into neighbours' houses and steals things.**
- **Shoplifts at the local department store.**

Certainly these illegal activities will affect your teenager's life. He or she is violating other people's rights and at the worst may do something to injure others. The young person is also learning about the law, probably first that it's easy to flaunt it, and then, if he or she is lucky, that it isn't so easy, that it can have very uncomfortable consequences. You cannot directly stop your son or daughter from doing these things, but if they keep it up, hopefully the police will intervene before they go much further. At that point your teenager may do a great deal of growing up – if you let it be his or her problem.

Sometimes parents hesitate to let the authorities discipline their children for lawbreaking because they think of being arrested as such a final, drastic event, and because they think that a 'record' can be damaging to a person later in life. Even if it were that bad we'd recommend putting this item on your kid's-life list, but it may be reassuring to you to know that a brush with the law is not usually that final nor drastic; most juvenile authorities are for adolescents not against them, and do everything they can think of to get them back into normal life without scars or permanent damage. Under the Rehabilitation of Offenders Act, a prison sentence if not for more than six months, and if the offence is not repeated, is wiped from the record after three years. If your son or daughter is experimenting with illegal activities, an encounter with the law without being bailed out by you may be the only thing that will save him or her. It would seem far better to undergo it now than later.

In short, we suggest you put these items on the kid's-life list. Aspects of this behaviour that you might hold out from this pile because they do affect you are:

> Having stolen goods in my house.
>
> Receiving calls from the police.
>
> Going to court with my son or daughter.
>
> Being charged for damages done by my teenager.

- **Wears revealing halters. Uses too much make-up.**
- **Has Mohican haircut (or shaves head).**
- **Wears scruffy looking clothes.**
- **He wears make-up and paints his finger-nails.**

The way a teenager dresses affects his or her life in many ways: in one sense it's a statement of how the young person sees him or herself, or wants to become, and it gives the outside world advance notice of what to expect of him or her. It doesn't affect your life; your way of dressing does that. Further, you have very little real control over how your teenager dresses except when he or she is right under your thumb. We'd suggest putting this one on the kid's-life pile, and reserve any aspects that do affect you, such as:

> Expects to go places with me, looking like a dropout, a tart, etc.

- **Won't do homework.**
- **Won't go to school.**
- **Is doing badly at school.**

What your teenager does about school certainly has an effect on his or her life – on what kinds of choices will be available in later days, the kind of work your teenager will do, the people he or she will mingle with, his or her self image. It is not basically a matter that affects your life; presumably you have already received whatever schooling you want, and have no need to repeat it through your child. Also, you probably can't make your teenager go to school nor perform well there. We haven't even seen it work when parents 'make' children do their homework. Thus, these school items might well go on the list of things that concern your teenager only. Aspects of them you might keep on your list if they bother you are:

> Letting me get phone calls from school authorities who blame me for my child's misbehaviour.

> Hanging around the house during school hours.

> Living in the house as a sponger, not pulling his or her weight. (In a sense, your basic deal with your teenager is probably that you provide the wherewithal for life support, and the teenager gets him or herself educated for adulthood. If he or she stops the education and still expects the support without substituting some other contribution, that's sponging.)

- **Lies around all day just eating and watching TV.**

This item doesn't sound like much, but it can be a constant irritant to a parent. It's often especially painful because the parent can't think of any good reason for not wanting the kid to lounge about, and thus must cope with feeling unreasonable and guilty as well as frantically annoyed.

In our experience this item is usually a secondary problem. The parent is usually feeling angry and helpless about other items and therefore has a hard time feeling good about anything their teenager does. If you feel taken advantage of, rejected, unfairly treated by someone, you are likely to have a negative reaction to everything about that person. Once those more basic problems are taken care of, it becomes easy to feel good about having that person around. We recommend working on those other, more basic items, and putting this one firmly on the kid's-life list, reserving aspects that do affect your life:

45

Eats up all the groceries.

Litters the house with dirty dishes and cigarette ends.

Prevents me from ever having any privacy.

This list may be enough to give you an idea of what kinds of items appropriately go on the kid's-life list.

There's a whole other group of problems that would seem to be kid's-life items but which we have nonetheless kept off that list. These are the items centering on things your son or daughter *says* or the *attitude* he or she expresses. In a sense, your teenager's lying, calling you names, or having a sullen or gloomy attitude need not affect your life unless you take it seriously. However, these items are not so appropriately handled through the approach we're going to recommend for the other items on this pile, and so we will not include them there, but will deal with them separately, later in the book.

The rest of the items remaining on our list (pages 32 to 33) can be seen to affect you directly, and will therefore be left on your original list as parent's-life items to be dealt with in the second half of this book.

Step Three

You now have a separate pile of things your teenager does that really do not affect your life. We're going to ask you to deal with these items in a certain, specific way which we will detail for you in the next paragraphs. However, *please do not carry out those instructions yet.* We recommend the following:

● Read through all of the instructions in the rest of this chapter.

● Then read through Chapters 3 and 4. They will help you develop a rationale for the way you interact with your youngster and give you a reservoir of confidence on which to base those interactions.

● Reread the instructions that follow in this chapter, carrying them out this time.

Basically, we're going to ask you to do two things about the items on the kid's-life list. *First, drop the responsibility for these items. Second, develop a trust that your teenager can and will make the right decisions in these matters for him or herself, and let him or her know you have that trust.*

You may find it fairly easy to do this, and if so, this one procedure can make a noticeable difference in the problems you're experiencing with your son or daughter. However, many parents find this step extremely difficult, and you may be one of them. If so, take it slowly, at your own pace. We don't want you to give up items too fast or too grudgingly, because if you have to force yourself too much you may give them up without letting go of the worry and resentment connected with them; that is, you won't be able truly to give them up at all. On the other hand, it's worthwhile to push yourself a little bit; the sooner you really give your child an item or two the sooner you will feel the relief and the benefits from it and the better you will feel about advancing even further.

Here is how you might go about letting these items go and learning to trust your teenager:

First: *Pick out the biggest item you can let go with any ease at all.*

Next: *Take a few minutes to practice giving it up in imagination first. Relax in whatever way helps you feel at peace with the world, and then go through the following sequence in imagination a few times:*

Imagine that you see your son or daughter doing this particular thing. As you do, you experience that old, familiar pang – a combination of worry, anger, and the helpless realization that, 'I've got to do something about that – and there's nothing I can do that will be effective.'

Then imagine that you remember that the responsibility for this behaviour is now going to be *not yours but your child's* and that you do not have to experience that pang any longer.

A feeling of relief and freedom from having had a weight taken off your back flows through you.

In that relief and freedom, if you feel like it, allow yourself to feel a new interest and curiosity in what the child might be doing – without your having to feel responsible for it. Let if be as though you were reading a book you like very much and that you know has a happy ending, but you have no idea what the next paragraph will be. With the security of the known happy ending, you can enjoy being surprised. When you can feel a friendly interest, imagine that you turn to your son or daughter and see that he or she is doing this thing from your kid's-life list. You notice this *with interest* and a basic feeling of trust that he or she will be able to work out the problem.

Now: *Rehearse a statement to your son or daughter in which you give him or her the responsibility for this item. It could go something like this:*

'Brian, I've been feeling worried and angry about you not going to school lately, and I've been trying to make you go.

'I've been thinking about it, and now I realize that's silly. I can't make you do anything, and besides it is your life that's affected, so it's really your business.

'I've realized you're quite able to make the right decisions about your school.

'From now on I'm going to stay out of your school decisions and trust that whatever you decide about school is right for you.

'I'm still interested and I'll do my best to help in any reasonable way, if you ask me, but basically, from now on it's your show.'

You may notice that this message has only six sentences, that 'I' is the subject of every sentence, and that there are no questions in the message. We call sentences of this sort *I-statements*. We'll talk more about effective speech patterns later in the book, and at this point simply ask you to follow suit as much as you can – make it a statement of what *you* feel and are going to do, not a statement telling your son or daughter what he or she could or should do. *Put what you have to say in I-statements, make it brief, and ask no questions* (such as, 'Why don't you want to go to school?', 'Would you like me to talk to your teacher for you?', 'Did you go to school today?' and so on).

Next: *Rehearse a brief statement of the reservations you have about this particular item. For example:*

'I am going to keep out of your school business; at the same time there are some things *I* want.

'I want the house clear of friends during school hours.

'I want to know everyone in the place is pulling his or her reasonable weight. I don't want to support a sponger.'

Notice again that this message is brief, and it is made up entirely of I-statements. It tells what *you* feel, what *you* want, what *you* are going to do. Make yours clear and short.

Practise your statement until you're quite comfortable with it.

Now: *Go to your son or daughter and tell him or her openly and directly that you have reached a decison about this particular item and what it is.*

Then: *Within the next few days or weeks, give him or her responsibility in a similar way for the remaining items on your kid's-life list.*

You may get a surprising response from your son or daughter when you say all this. We've seen children respond with everything from joy to tantrums, from accusations ('You don't care!') to exhortations to take back the responsibility, to apparent apathy and no discernible response. We recommend that you listen quietly to whatever your teenager says or does in response to your statement, and reiterate gently that this is what you want to do. Focus your attention not so much on the youngster's reaction as on your own resolve to stick with I-statements, to ask no questions, and to make it brief.

Parents too express a wide range of reactions to the very idea of doing what we suggest in this chapter. Some experience an immediate relief. Many others exclaim incredulously, 'Do you mean just let the child run wild?', 'Just let the child go?' Some express concern about being irresponsible themselves: 'That's giving up my job of being a guide', or, 'I'm responsible for my child!' Not infrequently a parent says something like, 'If I do that then he has won.' All of these responses are natural and understandable; they all stem from the parent's sincere attempt to do the best possible job of child-rearing. In the next chapter we'll look at why you may have had the reaction you did to the things we've suggested. Here we'll just say that if you do what this chapter recommends, you will have taken a major step towards resolving your problem. We say this regardless of how joyously or angrily or sullenly your son or daughter may have reacted to your statement or how hard or easy it may have been for you to do it. You've taken a first step at taking charge of your problem. Now the job is to follow through, building on this first step.

In Chapter 4 we'll deal with how the situation is likely to develop next and some ways of handling that development.

At this point you may be left with a number of items on your original list – things your teenager is doing that *do* affect your life. They're important, and we'll deal with them and with the aspects of the kid's-life items that you held in reserve, in the second half of this book.

Chapter Three

Why is it so hard to give your youngsters responsibility?

In the last chapter we asked you to do what professional therapists call 'giving up the control'. We know all too well that it may be much harder for you to understand or do this than it is for us to write about it. You may be having a great deal of difficulty even considering letting go the items on your kid's-life pile, and even if you're one of the parents who respond to these ideas with relief, you may be experiencing some doubts about the wisdom of it. What leads to these doubts and makes it so hard to do this?

We think we understand why it can be so difficult and even frightening to consider letting your child go to make his or her own mistakes. We think it's because you are trying to be a good parent, and have the idea that that means such things as the following:

> It's my job to see that my son or daughter turns out in a certain way and behaves a certain way. It's my job, for example, to see that he or she turns out to be honest, considerate to others, willing and able to work for a living, to have a good self-image and to use his or her potential. It's my job to see that he or she behaves in public, goes to school, eats properly, keeps clean, and so on.

> It's my job to guide my child. His or her job is to follow my directions.

> I'm obliged to care for my teenager. After all, he or she didn't ask to be born.

If my child gets into trouble, it's my job to bail him or her out of it.

It's right and proper for me to make sacrifices for my child because his or her needs and welfare are more important than mine.

It's my job to ensure my child's safety; I am the one who should be alert for dangerous situations, and protect my child from them.

It's my job to protect my child from suffering – from going through disappointments, mistakes and failures.

A great many parents in the world operate on a set of ideas something like these, and by and large it works; at least, large segments of the population brought up according to these ideas seem to survive and get along ostensibly all right. If you are having trouble with your teenager, you are probably a caring and conscientious person who is trying to apply some of these ideas in your family. That's why you are pushing your child to go to school, deciding he or she shouldn't see certain friends, making sure he or she has lunch money, clean clothes, and combed hair and all the rest of it. No one knows why these ideas 'worked' for so many other parents and children and may even be working for you and some of your children and aren't working for you and this particular one. It may be, though, that you are the lucky ones, that something in you and/or your teenager senses that there is something incomplete and therefore wrong about these ideas, and, without understanding it exactly, is pressing, through all this trouble, towards a different way. The very fact that you're having trouble may prove to be an opening for both of you to break through to a freer, more expansive, and much happier way of being, with a rejuvenated set of ideas.

What's wrong with the ideas above – apart from the important

fact that they're not working for you? We think that, basically, what's wrong with them is that they are based on some condescending and therefore destructive assumptions about what your teenager is and what you are. Over and over these ideas define your son or daughter only as a rather helpless being who cannot run his or her life but needs your direction, your support, the knowledge that you 'care' to keep him or her going. There's no mention of the young person as initiating anything or as competent to do his or her own thing. This is a very condescending view of your son or daughter. Meanwhile, these ideas define you not as a person who matters for yourself, but rather only in terms of your child's behaviour; you count only insofar as you're a 'good parent'. Your identity and value do not depend on anything *you* do, or are, but on what your child does or is. Your teenager's identity and value depend not on what he or she thinks or is like, but on how well he or she fits your expectations. Each of you is defined by the other and neither is a self-respecting and self-sufficient individual.

Certainly these assumptions contribute to a low self-image on the part of the young person; he or she is being told, in essence, 'You are not able to make good decisions; you are helpless and need another person (Dad and/or Mum) to think for you. Further, you are not responsible for what you do: Dad or Mum is!'

In a very deep sense these ideas break down your self esteem too. First, they set up a task for you at which you can only fail. It's as though on the one hand society said to you, through these ideas, 'You are a good person insofar as you are a good parent' and, 'A good parent controls his or her child'. Meanwhile, your common sense and the way your teenager actually behaves tells you, 'I cannot control my kid'. Thus the total message is, 'I must – and yet I cannot – control this person!' It's not surprising if you end up feeling frustrated, trapped and believing there's something wrong with you.

53

When a parent gets trapped in this pattern of thinking he or she may be doing an inappropriate parenting job for children of this age group. Even though few of us ever had formal training to be parents, we learned to control certain activities of our children for their own good. ('No, you can't go into the street with your tricycle.') Then, as our children matured, we tended to keep the old, progressively more inappropriate, control habits still in force 'for their own good'. ('No, you can't see Bill any more after he gets out of Borstal.') Playing in the street could be fatal for a child, whereas, for the adolescent, continuing to asssociate with Bill probably wold not be. In that sense you may be continuing habits of controlling your teenager which were appropriate when he or she was a child but which are no longer appropriate.

We are sometimes struck by the contrast between teenagers who rebel against this kind of parental control and those who don't. Sometimes the non-rebelling teenager comes to depend too much on parental decision making and reaches adulthood unprepared to carry on alone.

Ann's parents were extremely upset because of the way Ann (16) rebelled against their orders. She had been a model student but now was getting low marks and was interested in boys. The current crisis was precipitated by Ann's rebelling against her parents' orders to give up her job at Sainsbury's so she could spend more time on her homework. Ann's older sister (26) had, according to the parents, been a 'perfect' adolescent, never giving them any trouble. However, at 26 she had not been successful in keeping a job very long, wanted only to stay home and clean the house, and had no social life to speak of. As you might imagine, we suggested to the parents that their older daughter might have the more serious problem. By giving in to her parents' control, she had missed out on learning to take care of herself.

54

Thus, continuing the struggle to control your son or daughter's life, according to the ideas given on pages 51 and 52, may be giving you terrible trouble right now if you're failing in this control effort. If you're succeeding in your control, your teenager may be missing an opportunity to learn better self-responsibility.

Now, we're going to describe another philosophy – one that we believe would relieve some of the problems you are having and result in a more positive self image for both you and your son or daughter. It's not a set of ideas to be swallowed whole, but rather a few basic assumptions from which you can develop your own, individual ideas.

When a child is a baby, he or she needs a certain kind of caring in order simply to survive. A baby must be fed, washed, kept warm. So one kind of love you probably gave your child in early years was caring for his or her physical welfare.

Very soon, though, a baby begins to outgrow these physical needs – becomes able to crawl and then to walk, to feed, dress and wash him or herself, becomes able to take some responsibility for self and for the family. The small child's physical needs must still be provided for for a long time, but the need for this kind of caring diminishes steadily and is essentially outgrown by the teenage years and indeed, in some societies, by much earlier. We think that ideally you, the parent, outgrow your interest in giving it at the same time.

We think of this caring for the child's physical welfare as being on one level of love.

There is a second kind of love that a child and in fact every human being also needs in order to live. It is so essential that babies who do not receive it tend to die young. This is love which wants and cares about the inner being that the person most essentially is, the unique energy or initiative which animates the person. We could say it is love of the other person's *decision-making ability*. From the very beginning, your child came out with unique, individual ways of behaving that could have come only from him or her and that, taken all together, go to make up a totally unique person that you could never mistake for anyone else. Not only does he or she have a unique set of genes, not only is he or she physically unique, with unique fingerprints, but he or she has a completely individual way of doing things. He or she continually makes decisions that you could not predict, that could surprise you – decisions about what friends to make, what foods to prefer, what thoughts to think, and so on. *These individual responses are what you could most naturally love and enjoy about your child.* You miss out on them when you focus on what your child is doing that he or she 'shouldn't' do, or what he or she is not doing that 'should' be done. These individual responses come from a person's own inner being, the part that makes him or her a unique person. They are what tells us a person is alive rather than a doll or robot, and so your enjoyment of them can be called 'enjoying the signs of life.'

This enjoyment and wanting of another person's unique way of doing things and making decisions is what we mean by a higher level of love.

Giving your child this kind of love is the most important thing you can do for him or her. You have already been doing it at some level for many years. No matter how negative you may be feeling towards your teenager now, you could not be having any relationship with him or her at all if at heart you didn't care about each other as people. But this kind of love can also be nearly swamped by other ways of thinking or acting, mostly dutiful ones. Therefore we will talk about how you can give this kind of love to your teenager.

Basically, there are two ways in which to communicate this love, and they are both essential in getting you and your youngster out of your trouble. One way is what we call *modelling;* it involves letting your child see that you love and take care of your own inner being. We will talk about this in Chapters 6 to 10. The other is *actively wanting and encouraging your teenager's unique decision-making ability.* It's very probable that some of the things you do now which you mean to be helpful to your son or daughter actually function to belittle and block this ability. We ask you to switch your way of thinking around so that everything you do is directed to encourage and open ways for your teenager's decision-making ability. If you do that you will automatically be helpful to him or her at all other levels as well.

This is the main point we want to make in this chapter: that you may have been letting yourself feel good about your child only to the extent that he or she meets the standards of society; that insofar as this is so, you and the child are both being cheated; that you can learn, instead, to feel good about your youngster's unique decision-making ability.

Three distinct steps you can take in this direction right now are:

1. Notice and begin to drop any habit you have of making your teenager's decisions for him or her.

2. Learn to enjoy your adolescent's decision making.

3. Change some of your thoughts and beliefs about your son or daughter.

56

The work we suggest in Chapter 2, in which you give your teenager responsibility for the kid's-life items, gives you a good, basic start on the first step.

The second step, enjoying his or her decision-making more, has benefits for both you and your child. A person's inner being expands and develops when he or she is with people who treasure it and enjoy seeing it operate. You can give this to your teenager by realizing that here's a living, walking, talking piece of the most important show you could see in your life, and you have a precious but fleeting opportunity to see it and learn from it and enjoy it. It will take practice before you can get any enjoyment at all out of the upsetting decisions your teenager is making now, but if you drop the feeling that you are responsible for them, you may find yourself freer to notice the pathos and humour and humanness of the situation. A little piece of you may already be doing this; at the back of your mind there may sometimes be a twinge of surprise and amusement at the way you son is doing things, a little feeling of being touched by the naive and bumbling way your daughter is trying to find a place in the world, and a sense of how human and incongruous and vulnerable it all is. These feelings are your response to the touch of life and any little bit of them you experience is to be savoured and enjoyed.

A sense of perspective helps in learning to enjoy your teenager in this way. You might think back and recall some naive and bumbling things you yourself did when you were your child's age. Or

imagine that it's a neighbour's child who's acting the way your child is, and you are on the sidelines watching. Neighbours and other adults often get more enjoyment out of children and are better able to talk with them than the parents, and it seems to be precisely because neighbours do not feel responsible for making the kids' decisions. If the child is wearing scruffy clothes or spends hours watching television, the neighbour can simply notice this and wonder at the way the world goes – without saying, 'You should wear more respectable clothes', etc. Why shouldn't a parent take a similar attitude and become more free to enjoy his or her own child?

Without knowing it you may have always been approaching your teenager with the thought, 'She should be doing such and such; I'll see whether she's doing what she should', and 'I will approve or disapprove of what she's doing'. If you would like to enjoy your teenager more, try substituting the thought, 'I wonder what she's up to now?' with a very free feeling of curiosity and that you need not approve nor disapprove but can simply enjoy, as if you were watching a show. You will find that your son or daughter is surprising – and that one of the great rewards of being a parent is being able to enjoy these constant surprises. You will also find that sometimes you know more than your teenager does and can very well see that he or she is heading for some painful consequences, while the best thing you can do is simply state your apprehension and then let those consequences happen. In a way you're in the position of someone watching a caterpillar trying to get out of its cocoon. As a matter of fact, a real caterpillar has to struggle its own way out of the cocoon and in that sense 'suffer' if it is to be strong enough to beat its wings and fly; if it is 'helped' out of the cocoon it soon dies. Knowing this, an understanding parent can see a son or daughter make decisions that will obviously lead to pain, can let those decisions stand, and can still appreciate and enjoy the

humanness, the inevitableness, and the potential for new growth in the situation.

In short, for this step we want you to allow yourself to enjoy your kid's aliveness and unpredictability, even when the thing he or she surprises you with only dismays you at first.

If you'd like more specific instructions on how to enjoy your adolescent, try these exercises:

List for yourself ten things your child has done lately that are surprising or unexpected. Now for each one think of some aspect of the way the child did it that can give you a sense of pathos and amusement. Find some aspect of each incident that shows how naive your child can be, or which reminds you of something you did in the past, or which is so much your child's way of doing things that you recognize him or her in it. Find an aspect of which you can think, 'I understand why she did that!'

If you have difficulty thinking of these items, begin now to predict what he or she will do and say for the next five minutes at a time. Say something like 'I'm really interested in what is going on in your life' and see whether you were able to predict what his or her response would be. If you were able to predict accurately, enjoy the fact that you were right. If you weren't, enjoy the unpredictability and surprise of it!

Think of some things about which your son or daughter has been enthusiastic. Notice whether you get a little feeling of understanding and of wanting to see the kid get what he or she wants when you think of these things. This feeling, of wanting your child to have or be or do what he or she wants is a little piece of the love and enjoyment we're talking about.

The third step you can take to communicate love to your teen-ager, changing your thoughts and beliefs in a positive direction, is vitally important because of the powerful way in which people's beliefs interact with their actions. Without being aware of it, *we inevitably act toward making our inner beliefs come true.* Thus if you believe your child (or yourself) to be bad, helpless, or sneaky, you will also, without being aware of it, act to influence him or her (or yourself) to be just that. On the other hand, if you believe him or her to be basically good, to be able to make good decisions, and to be quite capable of running his or her life, you will inevitably and without effort have an influence in this direction. Even if you never say a word about it, a young person picks up your belief about him or her from the way you act, and because you are the parent, tends to take it seriously and to make it his or her belief as well. Then he or she begins acting to make it come true.

At this point you may be saying, 'But my little monster is doing these wrong things, making bad decisions right now. How can I change my view of that?'

Decisions generally have, from the decider's viewpoint, both good and bad consequences, some of which occur shortly after the decision is made, others which occur later. The more mature and experienced a person is, the more he or she pays attention to the longer range consequences. Thus adolescents tend to focus on the short term consequences while parents give greater consideration to the longer term consequences. This is in fact the source of much parent-adolescent conflict.

When a parent forces or tries to force an adolescent to decide in a certain way, the parent is generally focussing less on short term consequences and more on intermediate term consequences of the decision. However, there is an even longer term consequence that both parent and adolescent are ignoring, namely, *the learning, by the adolescent, to see all the consequences of a decision and to take them into account.* By learning to trust the child to make effective decisions, the parent achieves both the short term advantage of a conflict-free relation-ship with the child, and the longer range benefit of seeing his or her adolescent learn to see more clearly and to take account of longer term consequences of decisions. When the parent prevents (or tries to prevent) an adolescent from making a decision that has painful longer term consequences, the young person has fewer oppor-tunities to experience the negative consequences and even when he or she does, pays them little attention because of being so focussed on fighting the parent's control.

Thus, having faith in your son or daughter's ability to make good decisions can act to enhance his or her ability to do so. And your previous judgments about your kid's decisions may have been too narrow, considering your overall wants for your kid. For example, your daughter's decision to go shoplifting may have consequences which influence her later decision to be a person who doesn't steal, so that viewed from a larger perspective, it was a good decision!

We're saying that your underlying beliefs influence what you and your teenagers think of yourselves and put a limit on what you can do, be, have, in your lives. By changing those beliefs about yourself and your teenager, you can substantially influence what's happening in the total situation with him or her.

Here's a list of some beliefs parents often hold about their children, together with the kinds of reciprocal belief that their children are likely to develop:

Parent	*Teenager*
I am responsible for what my child does.	Dad (or Mum) is responsible for my actions; I am not responsible for what I do.
He won't make it.	I won't make it.
She can't make decisions.	I can't make decisions.
She's stupid.	I'm stupid.
He's mentally ill.	I'm mentally ill.
She's worthwhile insofar as she's 'good' – goes to school, conforms, is clean, polite, dutiful.	I am of worth for the way I fit in with what others want. Decisions I make for myself are not of value.
He can't take care of himself.	I can't take care of myself.

We want you to work on the way you think, and change every one of these to something positive. For example:

Parent	*Teenager*
My daughter is responsible for what she does.	I'm responsible for my own actions.
He'll make the best of whatever situation he's in.	Of course I'll make it.
She can make decisions.	Of course I can make my own, good decisions.

He's basically OK.	I'm OK.
I can trust him to take care of himself.	I can and I will take care of myself.
I don't know what he'll do next, but it will be really interesting to see what it is.	Mum's interested in me, and she trusts that I'll make decisions that are right for me.

If you are seriously interested in changing your thinking about your teenager from the first list to the second one, here is what we suggest you do.

Supply yourself with a small writing pad or some blank cards and a pen or pencil that you can keep with you for several days. Then, as you go through your day, notice how, every once in a while, you think about the situation with your teenager and experience a sort of pang because that situation is such a problem. Every time you get this pang, notice what kind of thought you're having about him or her. Don't be fussy or agonize about it; just notice the first thought that comes to your mind when you think about him or her. It may be something like, 'I hate this situation', 'Feeling sick about it', 'She's getting to me', 'This won't work', 'There's something wrong with him', or the like. Now get out your pad and pencil and write the thought.

Now write after it a new sentence, beginning with your son or daughter's name, and continuing, '. . .has everything she (or he) needs to make her (or his) own decisions and run her (or his) own life.'

Do this conscientiously for several days, until you notice that this thought pattern is becoming a habit; that is, that every time you feel a pang about the situation with your child, you're beginning automatically to follow it with the reassuring thought: 'My son (or daughter) has everything he (or she) needs to make the right decisions and to run his (or her) own life.'

. . . .

In this chapter we've been trying to make it easier for you to drop the responsibility you may have been carrying for decisions that your teenager can make about his or her own life.

Let's make it clear that we are *not* talking about encouraging your child to walk all over you, nor to disdain the 'shoulds' of society. That wouldn't work, if only because it would mean neglecting and even mistreating your own inner being. Neither are we suggesting you ignore your child or say you don't care ('Go ahead then, see if I care!') You can go on caring and being interested while refusing to take over any of your son or daughter's decisions.

We are talking about your seeing people as capable decision makers rather than as helpless, and doing everything you can to encourage your teenager to make his or her own decisions.

At this point parents often bring up to us a deep concern they have about what might happen if they 'let' their child make his or her own decisions in this way.

Isn't it dangerous?

She might go out and get raped, mugged, even killed.

He doesn't know how to handle himself; he'll get himself into real trouble if I don't guide him.

Their concern is certainly valid. Indeed there are dangers out there in the world, and youngsters – and other people too – do get raped, assaulted, even killed, every day. *All the more reason to aim toward making the kid responsible for his or her own behaviour as soon as possible.* The only real protection a young person has against these dangers is his or her own common sense and the knowledge that it's up to him or her to watch out for the dangers and make appropriate decisions about them. If your adolescent has the idea that worrying about dangers and making decisions about them is your job, he or she is likely to leave it to you and enjoy the carefree feeling of not being responsible. This is truly dangerous because he or she can then go out feeling that all sorts of things are safe because you are in the background and will pick up the pieces should there be any trouble. The fact is that you can't always be in the background nor pick up the pieces, so your son or daughter is operating on a very false feeling of security. Thus we think the best thing you can do towards really protecting your teenager against dangers is to drop the idea that it's up to you and let the kid know you are counting on his or her ability to make the right decisions for him or herself.

If you have the idea that you should wait to give a teenager this responsibility until he or she demonstrates an ability to take it, please reconsider. People do not necessarily learn to be responsible simply by getting older; you may know of people of thirty or forty who still will not take responsibility for their own lives. People learn to be responsible by finding themselves in situations in which they know they're on their own and making decisions for which they take the consequences. By protecting your child against the dangers of life you may be preventing him or her from developing the very strength it takes to handle them. We find that when children are really given full trust in their ability to run their lives, the ability to do just that suddenly shows itself in even the most unlikely young person. The lack of faith teenagers may show in their own ability seems related to lack of faith which others in their environment show to them.

If giving up efforts to control the different aspects of your child's life is still very difficult for you we suggest you give up whatever you comfortably can, pushing yourself just a little. Reserve the others for the time being. Perhaps later, as you see the positive results of doing what you can now, you will feel comfortable giving up more. Whatever you can do is likely to give long term benefits to you and your child.

Chapter Four

How your son or daughter may respond to all of this

In the last chapter we talked about an attitude of actually *wanting* to see your teenager make his or her own decisions. In this chapter let's work on what's likely to happen when you do hand over to your child the right to run his or her own life.

What is your son or daughter likely to do with this new 'freedom' if you decide to move out of the job of making decisions for him or her?

Most of the youngsters we see say that what they most want is more freedom to run their own lives. Given the urgency of this demand, one might expect that when they get it, they would respond with joyous faces and a happy smile. True, this does happen once in a while, but we have been amazed at how many children, when their parents finally agree to 'let' them make their own decisions, do not look happy at all. They're more likely to look glum, and to say things like, 'You don't care about me', 'You'll never live up to it', or even (and these are direct quotes): 'I'm not sure I'm ready to make my own decisions', and 'Please keep checking up on me!' And very often the first thing they actually do with the new freedom is to act even worse than they did before, in what is apparently in part an attempt to get the parents to take the control back.*

Let's see why they should behave in this way.

_____

* It is also in part a 'testing' of the parents' seriousness in dropping the control.

We think that an important part of every young person really needs and wants 'freedom' – wants to and can take charge of his or her life, make responsible decisions, and be his or her own person. *Another part is scared of this freedom, wants to be saved from it, and will do everything possible to get the decisions made somewhere else.*

This is far from just a child's problem; every human being is in this situation, all through life. Right from the start, we all want to 'do our own thing', and the same time want to pull back from it. Everybody wants to stand up and be definite and make his or her own life decisions, and also wants simply to stick with the safe old habits and let somebody else make the decisions. We're all a little like the circus lion in *Don Quixote* who longed to be free from its cage, out in the open plains. One day the cage door was accidentally left open, and the lion leaped out into the open. As soon as it did, however, the weight of all the freedom and responsibility it could now have came over it, and, in the story, it turned and *ran back into the cage.*

We all have the same kind of choice to make that the lion did, many times every day, between doing our own brave new thing and just going along with ready-made decisions. Probably most of us choose sometimes one way, sometimes the other, and most of the time manage a reasonably comfortable balance between these two ways. Generally we aren't even aware that we're constantly making this choice.

However, over and over again in our lives, things happen to make us re-think the way we've been choosing. Significant people enter or leave our lives, or we learn new things, or we graduate, or get married or have children. Every such change is a kind of crisis because it presses us to choose again, either to begin making more of our own decisions, or to let ourselves be run even more by the outside. It's never settled in a final way, because we keep getting new chances, over and over, to make the choice again.

It's probably clear that the writers of this book favour the decision-making choice over the use-the-ready-made-decisions choice. We think that ideally in human development a person becomes more and more able and willing to take over more and more of his or her own life decisions. That is what, psychologically, we call growing up, maturing, becoming responsible, becoming free, expanding one's consciousness. We know that both ways of choosing are important, and that everyone is inevitably going to make the use-the-ready-made-decisions choice many times, but in the long run hopefully the overall movement through all the 'crises' is towards taking the right to run one's own life.

If you're having trouble with your child, it's very likely that both of you are in this kind of crisis in which part of you wants very much to use your own head and run your own life, and another part is pressing you to fit in with ideas from outside yourself.

The teenager is in this crisis because he or she has reached an age at which, in this society, people begin establishing anew that they really are their own persons. When we look at the young person's situation, we see that up to about the age of eleven or twelve, he or she has been learning a great many new things, and probably in a large part *they've been your idea.* Even a child who objects vigorously all the way along probably learns much by modelling on you, the parent – learns to walk rather than crawl, to speak English, to use a fork and spoon rather than fingers, to dress rather than go naked, to go to school and many other things.

After all this has been learned, there comes a time for the child to learn the next big thing. This is to realize even more fully that he or she too can originate decisions, that he or she is a person separate from you or anyone else, a person who does run his or her own life. To stay healthy, the child *has* to realize he or she is not carbon copy, and that the impetus for his or her actions comes from inside him or herself and not from outside. In other words, it becomes important for the child to develop an identity of his or her own. To do so, the child must make some decisions that are different from yours, simply in order to realize he or she *can* originate ideas.

68

In our society the inner necessity for doing this usually hits children some time between eleven and sixteen. It's basically a healthy and positive thing and it means the child is growing and not that he or she hates you or is turning out badly. Later, after the youngster has gone through this and realized that of course he or she is a separate person, he or she may come back to you and end up following many of your ideas after all – but will then be doing so because he or she wants to, because it's his or her own idea, as an adult, to do so. *

Now, we want to emphasize what a frightening thing this inner pressure to make one's own decisions is for your child. He or she is in the position of the lion, for whom it was time to step out and make his own decisions, and who was also scared to do so. Certainly a part of the child honestly wants and needs to be free – and this is the direction of growth – but there is usually also a kind of

---

* It takes a higher level of maturity than most adolescents have to make a decision to do something that is right for them while a parent is insisting that they do *that same thing*. More usually they will 'show their independence' by doing the opposite, not realizing that in the process they are actually showing dependence.

panic at the idea of actually being free. The temptation is very great to run back into the cage, and most children do so many times.

The way children run back into the cage is by *getting someone else to make decisions for them.* The sequence is something like this:

1. The daring thought occurs to the child of making a responsible decision of his or her own.

2. A feeling of panic comes over him or her.

3. The child does something that he or she knows will provoke you, *in order to get you to make the decision.*

4. You respond by telling him or her how to behave – supervising, scolding, approving or disapproving, and so on.

If the child can accomplish this – get you or someone else to say how he or she should behave, to supervise, to approve and disapprove – then the child does not have to do it. He or she is safe from having to make self-decisions. Now, having set someone else up as the bossy decision maker, the child can resent being 'dictated to', insist loudly upon wanting freedom, and meanwhile do as he or she pleases without having to feel responsible.

Going through this sequence over and over again is not as comfortable a position as it may sound and the morose and sullen expressions of many of our acting-out teenagers may reflect the way it actually feels. It's an uncomfortable position because the youngster can never make it complete. Something in him or her knows it is not meant to live in a cage, simply obeying or defying other people's decisions, that it is meant to be free and make self-decisions, and this something keeps prodding the person from the inside. Things keep coming up that push the teenager to consider leaping to freedom again by making a responsible decision. However, this would be like leaping out of the cage; the very thought brings on the feeling of panic again, and so the teenager quickly puts the idea down. He or she does so by once again provoking you or someone else to take over the controls – doing something that will get you to scold or punish, to approve or disapprove, to question, to supervise, to tell him or her what to do and what not to do. Once you do respond in this way, life is safe again, back in the cage – probably unhappy, but at least safe. However, it doesn't last; before long the idea of running his or her own life pops up again. The cycle keeps repeating itself, and the teenager has to manipulate you again and again to keep you on his or her back.

Almost always both of you are unaware of operating according to this pattern, and wouldn't know what we were talking about if we asked why you do it. Yet the chances are high that a good bit of this is going on between you.

We could say that the teenager has worked him or herself into an addiction to negative attention. Every time the possibility of making his or her own responsible decision comes up, your son or daughter responds by provoking *you* to take the responsibility instead, and you do so by looking at him or her in one way or another with negative attention, which says, "I say you should do so and so." Without necessarily being aware of it, most teenagers nevertheless understand very well what things will bother their parents and how to use these things to provoke just the degree of advice, punishment, restriction or disapproval they're looking for. In one family the daughter does it by staying out late or calling the parent names; in another the son does it by saying the parent doesn't care or by refusing to take baths. One teenager we knew did it by assuming a very innocent air and then asking her father questions like, "Dad, what do you think about girls who get pregnant?" At that time she had no interest in becoming pregnant, nor was she honestly curious about what her father thought (she already knew), but this kind of question got her just the right amount of startled and upset attention to assure her that her father was still acting as her watchdog and she did not have to be responsible.

In order to stay in the down-trodden, abused position negative attention provides, youngsters will not only provoke negative attention from you and from authorities in general; they also make the most of what they do get by exaggerating it, and even invent it wholesale if they have to. Many are the teenagers who confide to friends the cruelty, strictness, or uncaringness of what the world would consider perfectly reasonable parents; to be able to describe the worst mistreatment becomes a rather glamorous thing to do among teenagers. A young person achieves safety, in the sense we're speaking of here, by setting him or herself up as a desperate, misunderstood character. Since you can't really be a desperate character without a villain, the teenager must then provoke whoever he or she can (probably you!) to take the role of forbidding dictator. And once is not enough; the teenager must keep on provoking you in order to maintain you and him or herself in these roles. Some of the hassles between you and your kid may have been more basically 'about' the child's attempt to get you to take that forbidding stance again than 'about' the issues you thought you were arguing about.

We are suggesting that many of the disturbing things your teenager does are done not because they're so much fun nor because he or she hates you, but are done *in order to get you to give negative attention and thereby save the child from having to make his or her own responsible decisions.* In a sense the child is addicted to negative attention as if to a drug, and you are in the position of supplier. We would go even further with the analogy and say that the drug is a harmful one; your negative attention actually encourages the child to continue evading making his or her own responsible life decisions.

In short, what the young person has probably been *getting* at this time in his or her life is negative attention – scolding, disapproval, worried advice, messages of despair at how he or she is turning out, ever more desperate attempts to control him or her. What he or she *needs* in this situation is help and encouragement to make the make-my-own-decisions choice.

You may well have been in something like this pattern with your teenager. Now, in this book, we're asking you to stop trying to control the decisions that really belong to your son and daughter. In accord with this pattern, he or she is very likely to respond at first by trying to provoke you into taking the controls back. He or she may do any of the things we've listed on page 21 or may step up activity in the very areas in which you have just given 'freedom', or may come up with some completely original provocative behaviour.

We want you to be comfortable about handling such flare-ups, so we ask you to prepare for them ahead of time by studying the recommendations we will make about what you can do if your son or daughter reacts in this way. First, though, realize that the more prepared and relaxed you are about the possibility of getting such reactions, the less intense they are likely to be. In situations in which parents have begun to drop the controls as we're asking you to do in this book, children do less trying out and provoking of the parents, the more sincere and wholehearted the parents are in actually dropping the controls. The more firmly you are committed to following through on what you started in Chapter 2, the sooner the children seem to realize you do mean it, realize you actually want them to take care of themselves, and begin to do so.

Here, then, are some ways you might act if and when your teenager seems to behave worse than ever after you have dropped your control over the kid's-life items.

When you become aware that the behaviour that has troubled you is going on, your first reaction may be a flash of anger, disappointment, frustration. If so, STOP – refrain from saying or doing anything about the behaviour while you consider the following ideas.

a. Your experiencing this anger, disappointment or frustration is the first step in giving your teenager the negative attention he or she is hooked on but should not have. If you go ahead and express it further it may only reinforce the teenager in irresponsible behaviour.

b. The teenager is not doing anything to *you* by this behaviour. (Remember, we are still talking only about the kid's-life items.) This behaviour affects his or her life, but not yours. How about letting the anger, disappointment and frustration that may go with that behaviour be his or hers too? Relax, re-assure yourself and get back a long range perspective on the situation.

If it helps you to drop the anger, etc., try imagining that it is a friend or an aunt or uncle of yours who is behaving in this way, instead of your child. You may find yourself taking it less personally, and feeling sorry, surprised, perhaps concerned, that this other person has this problem – rather than angry or frustrated.

c. It's true that your teenager seems to be pushing you to take over control from the outside again, but just as certainly there is a part of him or her that wants and needs to be set free of it. Trust that that part, the aspect of your son or daughter that is very well able to make good decisions, is there ready to take over when all this trouble between you is over.

Whatever your first impulsive feeling about the behaviour may be, *stand firm in your decision not to take back the controls.* When the behaviour happens, you may feel an immediate urge to respond as you are used to doing – by feeling sorry for the youngster, expressing alarm, asking questions, shaking your head, giving advice.

DON'T. No doubt you will slip up a few times – perhaps many times – before you completely overcome the habit of trying to control your teenager, but begin again as many times as you need to until you can do it. Think of your negative attention to your son or daughter as a dangerous drug, and refuse to continue dispensing it.

What to do instead:

Remain friendly and courteous in your manner with your teenager. Since you have previously been the supplier of negative attention, it's important that you now supply something very different. The two crucial elements of negative attention are that (1) it's negative, and (2) it's usually highly charged. An attitude that's generally accepting and at the same time relaxed and low key will provide a good antidote. Keep remembering: 'I'm doing very well; it's this other person who has a problem', and, 'This person has not done anything to me.'

Generally, keep your attention focussed on your own activities, so that you are not even alert to notice whether or not the child is doing these things that affect only him or her. When you do notice that the behaviour is happening, do nothing about it until and unless 1) You haven't been able to drop it from your mind and still feel bothered by it, or 2) It is brought to your attention in a very clear way – that is, until your son or daughter tells you about it directly, or does it right in front of you, or someone else – police, school teacher, neighbour – tells you about it. Do not play detective, ferreting out how your son or daughter is behaving.

When you do get a clear message that behaviour that troubles you is happening, talk with your teenager if you want to, but do it in a special way – a way in which you keep responsibility for your own behaviour while refusing to assume responsibility for their behaviour. You can do this by using mostly I-sentences, sentences telling what you think, feel, want, will do, so that in a sense, the focus is on you rather than your son or daughter.

Here is a sequence of things you might incorporate into what you say instead of the negative attention responses you used to make. Use any of them that feels right for you.

1. Make clear in one sentence what you're talking about. If the behaviour has come to your attention in some way other than your child telling you directly, tell him or her what it is.

> The education welfare office phoned today to say you had not been at school for ten days.

> I notice you're riding on your friend's motorbike with no helmet.

> The police tell me you were taken to the Police Station for being drunk and disorderly.

Say how you are feeling about this situation – in an I-sentence.

> I am concerned to hear about it.

> I feel sad about this.

> I'm worried when I hear this.

> I'm surprised.

3. Point out any consequences you see.

> It seems to me if you do this, the consequences will be such and such.

If you're quite anxious about the behaviour, tell your youngster the fantasy you have about what may happen. It's fine to play this up; it may even help you to exaggerate it to absurd lengths. As long as you stay responsible for the fantasy (by presenting it in terms of I – as your thinking) it won't hurt your kid nor provoke him or her into actually fulfilling it.

> I'm imagining you'll leave school and go out on the streets and get raped and not be able to get a job and end up on the dole.

I'm afraid you'll go out on the motorbike and have an accident and be hurt and go to hospital and have to be operated on and have permanent brain damage and become a vegetable.

4. Acknowledge your helplessness while disclosing what you wish your son or daughter would do.

I want you to finish sixth form college, and I know I can't control you.

I'd like to see you in by ten o'clock, and I know I can't make you do anything.

I'd like to see you decide against smoking pot, although I know I'm helpless to make that decision.

5. If it's appropriate and you really want to, remind your teenager once that you're willing to help if he or she wishes. Then, if your child does ask you to help, make sure you merely give him or her a hand and do not take the situation over. Enquire as to exactly what would be helpful and then confine yourself to it. Let any further ideas come from him or her. If no more help is asked for, stay out of the situation.

6. (And this is a very important step): State your belief that your son or daughter can and will make the right decisions for his or her life.

I know you'll make the right decision for you.

I'm sure you'll come up with a good solution.

I know you've got what it takes to work it out in the long run.

The full message you might give, then, when you notice your teenager doing something that's his or her business and which nonetheless worries you, is something like this:

I see from this school report that you're doing badly this term. I feel sorry about that, but I know you'll work out the best way to handle it for yourself. Let me know if I can help.

I notice you're using marijuana quite a bit. I keep imagining you'll become a burnt out shell and injure your brain and lose the ability to do athletics and schoolwork. I wish you'd stop, although I know I'm helpless to make you do anything. And I know you'll make the right decision, whatever it is, for yourself.

Your kid may do some things that result in outside pressure on you to intervene. For example, neighbours may complain to you about noise made by your son or daughter; the school may hold you responsible for damage; the police may phone you in the middle of the night to tell you that your son has been arrested and that you should collect him from the Police Station.

In these situations the young person has, in a sense, enlisted society to pressure you into taking over responsibility for him or her. It would be best not to give in even to this pressure. Do what you feel is right for you to do under the circumstances calmly, without yielding to the pressure to scold, blame, question, ignore your child, or that other pressure, to feel guilty because your child did something wrong. This will be hard for you, and we do not mean to treat it lightly. It may help to plan in advance what you will do if you get phone calls like this. The way you find out about your teenager's misbehaviour may catch you by surprise, and it may be helpful to tell yourself in advance, 'Whatever happens, I will calmly and deliberately take what seems like the best action without yielding to the pressure to do immediately what someone else seems to want me to do.'

If you stay relaxed, it may even be possible to use this kind of situation to advantage, to demonstrate that you do indeed see your teenager and not yourself as responsible for his or her actions. When the neighbour phones, for example, try putting your kid on the phone and let him or her work out a way to make things right. If the school authorities report to you that your daughter is misbehaving, tell them you give them your full permission to do whatever they do with children who behave in that way, and simply deliver their message to your daughter. If you receive an ominous looking letter from the school addressed 'to the parents of' your son, hand that letter to him saying something like, 'I believe this is for you, Bob.' If the police tell you to collect your son or daughter from the Police Station, arrange to do so when it's convenient for you; don't leap out of bed to do it, nor interrupt your working schedule. In these ways you tell the young person that you care enough about him or her as a decision-maker that you are not going to bail him or her out, and the consequences of your teenager's own behaviour will fall not on you but on his or her competent shoulders.

What should you do if your teenager does something extreme that is potentially harmful to him or herself or to others – gets involved in unusually excessive use of alcohol or drugs, makes a serious suicide threat or attempt or seriously threatens harm to others? This, we think, becomes a special case. When young people do things that could so obviously lead to their being arrested or taken to a hospital, we assume that they need the outside controls more than they need the freedom for the time being – controls firmer than you could give them, that they can't break. The principles we are talking about in this book apply to these children just as to any others, but we feel that the element of physical danger makes these situations too tricky for you to handle alone. These children have often already become involved with some kind of authority that can provide a situation with limits – police and probation officers, with doctors and so on. In these situations we suggest you make the fullest use of what these people can do in the way of setting limits for your son or daughter. Working through the programme in this book would be an excellent *additional* approach for you to take in trying to bring up teenagers who do this kind of acting out.

On a short-term basis, then, when you hand over responsibility for personal decisions to your teenager, you can expect anything from immediate improvement in the situation to flare-ups of even worse behaviour than you started with. Don't be afraid of these possible flare-ups. If you're ready for them they need not be frightening, and if you're firm and sincere about really transferring responsibility for personal decisions over to your teenager, they are likely to be brief. When they're over, if you stick to what we have suggested that you do, we think you have every right to look forward to a more rewarding and comfortable situation than you had before.

One last bit of advice to you as you work on applying these ideas: *Do not give up*. The approach we're suggesting is powerful – more powerful than it may sound at first, and sometimes using it will resolve situations for parents and teenagers almost immediately. In many other cases it takes longer. You may be one of the parents who sees little or no change either in your teenager or in yourself for some time, even though it seems to you that you're doing everything we've talked about. It's important that you stick with it and be alert to instances in which, without realizing it, you are still doing things in the old way. In this approach you're working for a change in an overall way of looking at things, for you and your son or daughter. You can do a lot to move in the direction of that change by doing all the small things we suggest in this book, but there's also a sense in which you have to grow into it. Also, you and/or your teenager may simply have to go through more hassle, may have to hit bottom, as it were, before the situation begins to reverse. So persevere and be prepared to be thorough and persistent in applying these ideas. Assume that everything you're doing that we've talked about *is* helping, and that the positive results will accumulate to a reasonably happy ending – whether or not you see benefits immediately. We know from the many desperate parents we've worked with that it can happen.

Chapter Five

Breaking the mutual safety arrangement

We've talked now about several factors that may be making it difficult for you to drop your control over the kid's-life items. In Chapter 3 we looked at some ideas you may have had about how a good parent should act. In Chapter 4 we looked at how your teenager may be getting safety out of your efforts to control and how he or she may actually do things in order to *provoke* that control.

After all this, however, you may still be having some difficulty in giving up the idea that it's your job to control your son or daughter. Why?

Let's look at what controlling your teenager does for *you*. Because strangely enough, much of what we said in the last chapter about the child's fears of doing his or her own thing and the use of outer controls to save him or her from it is very likely to apply to you as well.

We've said that the business of having to choose between doing your own thing and using the ready-made decisions does not apply just to teenagers. It goes on all through life – *including the point you are at now*. In fact, it seems to us it may be especially acute for you at this particular time of your life.

Difficulty in making this choice comes to a peak at certain crucial times of our lives. Adolescence is one. The time when one's offspring leave childhood and begin entering adulthood is another.

This is a natural crisis time for you because right now a change in your identity is impending. For years a part of that identity has been the idea, 'I'm a person who's responsible for bringing up children.' However easy or hard that has been for you, you've at least become used to it; it's familiar. Now hints are reaching you that a different way of living is on the way. Your child doesn't need you in the same way he or she used to, and *that frees you* – for who knows what new possibilities? It's as though the cage door has swung open and a changed situation, with all its pluses and minuses, is waiting for you. There's a new freedom out there; things are going to be different and *you* will be deciding how your life will be then. This prospect of change and new freedom has been there all along as your relationship with your child changed from babyhood to adolescence, but it takes on a greater vividness when your child gets this close to adulthood, and this makes your situation a crisis. You may very well experience the two feelings the lion did: 1) an eagerness to jump into the new and different life, and 2) a reluctance, scaredness and sadness about it.

We are writing very seriously about this crisis and the difficulty for you of choosing between your own original ideas and ready-made ones. What we've described may not seem to fit your situation exactly, but if you are feeling troubled in some way, it's very likely that at some level you are indeed becoming aware of new possibilities of doing your own thing and are also a little afraid of them. The wish for something to save ourselves from our own new possibilities is often very strong.

Now, you may remember we said that adolescents, who are in the same kind of position, save themselves from doing their own thing by trying to get others to take over control of them. Adults do this too.

Let's look at how this works. People save themselves from doing their own things by, first of all, *thinking* in a certain way. It is a four-step thought sequence, and it goes as follows:

1.) The first step is to experience the beginning of *a daring thought*. An idea occurs to you of something you might like to do, or be, or have.

I might . . .

> go into politics.
> become an anthropologist . . . a dancer!
> drive to the beach this afternoon.
> get myself a new coat.
> take up fencing . . . (or Swahili . . . or embroidery . . .)
> take a nap . . .
> feel happy!

2.) Second is a *sensation of panic* – or at least something we interpret as panic and act upon as if it were panic. Often very tiny, hardly noticeable (because we so quickly get rid of it), it can also be overwhelmingly strong. It is definitely related to the daring thought; it says about it, 'Dangerous!'

3.) The third step is to *think of something that makes the first step impossible.* It starts with a phrase like, 'But I can't because . . .', 'If I didn't have to . . .', or 'If it weren't for . . .' and then adds something that limits you.

> But I can't because:
>> there's no time.
>> I don't have the right clothes.

> If I didn't have to:
>> do the dishes.
>> support a family.
>> earn a living.

> If it weren't for:
>> my spouse.
>> my children.
>> expenditure cuts.
>> the way I was brought up.

And so on.

This is the step in which you pick out some factor and set it up as controlling, or limiting you. This step cancels out the daring possibility of Step 1, and makes you feel safe again.

4.) The fourth step is a *feeling of frustration which you experience as having to do with Step 3*, even though a psychotherapist might see it as more truly stemming from disappointment that the beautiful, daring thought of Step 1 is being rejected. At this point, then, you have some not-so-pleasant feeling 'about' the item in Step 3:

Resentment.

Unhappiness.

Worry.

Guilt.

Depression.

A trapped feeling.

And again, this frustrated feeling can be of any intensity, from very mild to nearly overwhelming. It serves to shore up and maintain Step 3 *in order to keep the daring thought safely smothered*, and it is exactly as intense as it needs to be to accomplish this. Thus, the more intense this unpleasant feeling, the more intense and daring we assume the original Step 1 thought to have been.

The complete sequence, then, goes something like this:

Maybe I could do my own thing. But that's worrying. Aha! I see that I can't do my thing because of this limiting factor. How frustrating that limiting factor is!

As far as awareness goes, however, we tend to gloss over and forget the first two steps and remain very much aware of the last two. This makes sense, for these last two steps have only one reason for being. They are *designed* exactly to keep you in such impasse, pain and conflict that you can't remember and certainly can't act upon Thought 1. Thus you end up being aware only of: 'I'm so frustrated by this limiting factor!'

Now, if you are dissatisfied enough with this kind of experience, it is possible and desirable to work your way back to the first thought and start the whole thought sequence again, in the direction of fulfilling it somehow rather than crushing it. We'll talk more about ways of doing this in the next chapter. Right now, we want to consider what kind of thing you may be doing in your Step 3.

People can choose anything they like to fill in Step 3, whether or not it makes sense or is appropriate. Actually, nothing they pick is going to be really appropriate anyway, because the whole thought sequence is irrational. In practice, we all tend to pick whatever factor is most convenient, and blame our failure to do our own thing on it. And in families, parents are one of the factors most convenient for children to use for Step 3, and *children are available for parents.*

In other words, if you're like most parents, it's very tempting to use something about your child or the way he or she behaves in Step 3 in order to save yourself from doing your own thing.

> I can't
>> enjoy myself
>> do what I'd like
>> have some privacy
>> be an artist
>
> because
>> my teenager won't behave and it's my job to see that he or she does.

We're suggesting, in short, that you may be saving yourself from doing your own thing by trying to control your child. *This safety from your own deepest wishes is what you can gain by trying to keep the controls over your child, and that's another big reason why it's so hard to drop those controls.*

Meanwhile, you may recall from Chapter 4 that the child is getting safety from doing his or her own thing by pushing you to take over control. It begins to look very much like a *mutual* arrangement in which each of you saves the other from being free to do your own, original thing.

Unfortunately, we think each of you does more for the other than simply saving him or her. *You pass the fear onto each other,* too. People's attitudes are contagious. When you see someone who's unafraid, you're likely to feel more able and courageous too, and when you

see someone cowering in fear, you're likely to experience a pang of fear yourself. As long as you and your child are in this arrangement, each of you is showing the other that you are afraid of doing your own thing, and, in a sense, you pass that fright on to the other. Each is giving the other the message:

It's unsafe to do one's own thing.
Self-initiated behaviour is dangerous and frightening.
It's safer to go along with other people's opinions, commands, ideas, than with one's own.

Each is telling the other, 'You should not run your own life.' The parent's behaviour says to the child:

You should be run by me, *not by yourself*.

The child's behaviour says to the parent,

You should run me, *not yourself*.

Thus not only do parent and child save each other from doing their own things, but each influences the other to be even more afraid of Step 1 thoughts.

This mutual safety arrangement usually develops into a routine in which both sides have definite parts and act them out over and over again on cues from each other. The kid usually has the roles of being rebel and fugitive, telling lies, conning the parent, feeling unjustly dominated. The parent has the roles of giving orders, interrogating, presenting explanations and lectures the adolescent has already heard before, playing detective, scolding and punishing, and feeling cheated, frustrated, worried.

Mandy (15) misses school to smoke pot with friends. Her mother scolds, pleads, or punishes. Mandy feels bad and guilty and says she won't do it again. Mother feels relieved. Three days later Mandy misses school to go swimming with friends. Mother scolds, pleads or punishes. Mandy feels bad and agrees to go to school. The next week she misses school to go and wander around the shops.

Dave (14) steals money from his mother's purse. Mother feels frustrated and worried and lectures him about morality. Dave cries and agrees to reform. Mother leaves her purse lying around the house. Dave steals from it. Mother lectures him. Dave says he will change his ways.

Jackie (16) comes home late for supper. Her father feels hurt and asks her why. She says she didn't have a watch. He explains lengthily that she could use friends' watches or hear the time on the radio. A few days later she comes home two hours late for supper. He asks her why, gets angry, keeps her in for a week. She explains she was in a car that broke down. A week later, she is again late but 'just happens' to be seen walking past the house in the direction of the local park about fifteen minutes after suppertime. Her father goes out to look for her and can't find her. When she does arrive, father interrogates her, keeps her in again and feels extremely frustrated.

We're saying that *all* of the behaviours in these examples, both of parents and teenagers, actually *serve* to *keep* both parent and teenager in a desperate, struggling situation. Of course, no parent sees it this way while running through these routines, any more than the child does. You don't purposely decide you're going to perpetuate a miserable situation for you and your son or daughter just for the fun of it. You run through these responses automatically, and are not aware that you are actually keeping the situation going as it is by saying and doing exactly what you are. You are playing a ping-pong game while in a stupor; in actual fact you're one-half responsible for keeping the game going by continuing to hit the ball back, but *you don't know you're doing it.* We want you to wake up from the stupor, become aware that your responses do influence the way things go, and take responsibility for running your side of the game according to the way you want it to go.

The four-step habit of thinking we're talking about in this chapter can be changed; it's a possible and basically straightforward task to learn to think differently, and your doing so would be beneficial for both you and your child. It's clear that thinking without so many limitations would free you to fulfil more of your own, unique possibilities in life. At the same time, if you were thinking in a more effective way, you would be giving your child a model of courage. Since courage is as contagious as fear, you would be influencing him or her to be courageous too, and to use his or her own decision-making ability just as you would be using yours.

We'll be talking further about ways of thinking more effectively. Straight away, though, to begin getting yourself out of whatever Step-3 use you may have been making of your son or daughter, we suggest you do the following:

1. Sit down and, taking your time, *decide what you would best like to do if you were given an absolutely free half hour every once in a while* – a half-hour during which there were no demands upon you excepting only that you were to enjoy and feel free in what you did. A half-hour just for you, with *no demands* – how would you spend it? Here are some answers parents we worked with have come up with:

> Work with my macramé that I haven't touched for months.

> Lie in a deck-chair and just enjoy doing nothing.

> Go to the library and browse around.

> Cook something nice and eat it.

> Potter in my workshop.

> Soak in the bath with a good mystery story.

> Take a drive.

Make sure that the thing you decide on is something you enjoy simply because it's fun for *you*, and that it's something you can make happen all by yourself so that you won't be dependent upon anyone else's wanting to join you or set things up for you.

2. When you have picked something, do whatever has to be done to make it completely convenient for you to jump into this activity on the spur of the moment. If the activity is wood carving or macramé, see that the tools and supplies are laid out ready to hand, so when the time comes you can begin enjoying without the delays

of getting ready. If it's reading, obtain the books or magazines you want and put them in a convenient place so you can get at them at a moment's notice. If it's going to the library, make sure you know the library hours and plan something just as appealing for the times when it's closed.

3. Now *promise yourself* that the next time – and every time – you have a Step-4 feeling (frustration, anger, worry etc.) about something on your kid's-life list, you will not make yourself suffer by dwelling on it or by engaging in a hassle about it, but will instead *use this feeling as a signal* that you are to spend the next half-hour on this selected activity.

4. Now do just that.

It could go something like this:

Bill's father has lectured Bill (14) on productive use of his time, but Bill persists in watching television three or four hours a day. Now, Father walks in, sees that Bill is again sprawled in front of the TV, experiences a pang of dismay about it — and turns on his heel to go and spend half an hour in the garden, where he is experimenting with different kinds of compost.

Karen (16) has run away and is staying with friends her mother emphatically disapproves of. She is in misery because she feels a pang of dread every time she thinks of Karen or hears the phone ring or a car approach the house. Then she remembers this exercise. The next time she experiences this pang, she listens to it and does something to make it feel better: she gets in the car and goes window shopping at the local shopping centre.

While she's making dinner, Anne's mother gets a phone call from the school telling her that Anne (13) has not been at school for two weeks. She experiences a pang of worry, anger, frustration. She turns to Anne and says, 'It's a message for you — the school just called to say you had not been there for two weeks. I get a pang of worry when I get a message like that, and I want to make myself feel better. Therefore I'm going to take a bubble bath and read my new magazine.' She turns off the stove and disappears into the bathroom.

Sometimes you may get your Step-4 feeling at a time that is not convenient for you to take a half-hour for yourself. You may be in the middle of an important business conference, or nursing a baby or studying for an exam of your own. At times like this, the activity you've set up ahead of time may no longer be what you most want to do with a free half-hour; you may *want*, instead, to continue with what you were doing. When this happens, first promise yourself the original half-hour, and at some specific time, very soon ('as soon as, this conference is over', or 'at 7 p.m. tonight') and be resolved to keep this promise. Then allow yourself immediately to become engrossed in your important current activity and to *enjoy* it. The aim here is double; it is to *take care of yourself by seeing to it that you enjoy what you are doing*, and it is to *abstain from focussing negative attention on your son or daughter*. We recommend, also, that you be as ruthless as you possibly can in deciding which activities you will interrupt in order to take your half-hour. Even if you're in the midst of something the whole family depends on when you get your Step-4 feeling, there's a good chance it would do more for them (*and* you) to see that you will take care of yourself when something hurts you than to see you dutifully continuing in some 'should' activity for them.

In these last four chapters we have been asking you to drop your controls over your teenager, and we have described the kinds of problems you may run into when you do this. Now we want to talk about some advantages of doing so. One of them, of course, is the beneficial effect on your child. Another important one is this: that as you begin to succeed in dropping controls over your youngster's life, you may become aware of an odd sort of feeling about doing so. You are dropping something you've been used to for a long time, an old habit, and it may feel strange to you to be without it. People sometimes experience this feeling as a kind of 'space' within themselves, a sense almost of a vacuum. Others describe a new sense of lightness. It may be a feeling as if a mountain had fallen off your back, or as if something you were used to had been lost, leaving a kind of emptiness. If you do not know what this feeling is, it can be worrying, even frightening, but we'd like to see you learn to value it. In this feeling you may be experiencing *the space in which you can do your own thing*. In its unfamiliarity it may be a little frightening but, even more, it is precious and extremely important for both you and your teenager.

It is in the sense of finding this lost space for yourself – the space in which you can bring your own previously smothered wishes to fulfilment – that the whole problem with your teeanger can actually turn out to be a positive thing for you. That problem may turn out to have been the exciting factor which got you to take care of and fulfil your own daring possibilities, while at the same time encouraging your teenager to make the most of his or hers.

At this point, if you've read through and thought about this chapter and Chapters 3 and 4, and have done the things we have asked you to do, you're ready to make a formal handing over of the controls for his or her life to your son or daughter. Go back to pages 47 to 49 of Chapter 2 to do this. Then proceed to Chapter 6, in which you begin to lay the groundwork for dealing with the parent's-life items by learning to take back responsibility for your own happiness.

Chapter Six

Taking back responsibility for your own life

Let's begin now to prepare for your successful handling of the rest of the items on your list, the parent's-life items. In this chapter and the next we'll work to help you develop the basic attitude that will enable you to do that. It's an attitude we call 'taking care of yourself', by which we mean that you respect, care about, and can be counted on to be loyal to your own inner self.

If you are experiencing trouble, either because of something your son or daughter is doing or for some other reason, it is almost certain that, in one way or another, you have not been taking care of your own wants and needs. Without being aware of it, you are ignoring a voice from within yourself.

Everyone has a signal giver inside, an inner being which is constantly sending him or her daring thoughts:

I feel . . .

I want . . .

I might . . .

I can . . .

I will . . .

I'm going to . . .

Ideally, there is a strong, positive relationship between you and this inner signal-giver. You hear it, respect and care for it, and trust it to guide your behaviour – and it in turn is trustworthy. It can be seen as your primary task in life, to fulfil this inner being of yours.

However, many of us learn very early in life to ignore, even fear, this inner voice. We change so we do not even hear it, and instead develop the habit of focussing on messages from outside ourselves to guide what we do.

Most of the ideas of what a 'good parent' does were like this; they came from society, not from yourself, your own common sense.

It's not uncommon for ignoring one's own inner voice to become such a habit that a person becomes able to hear and take care of what other people need, but does not hear nor pay attention to his or her own wants and needs.

A capable executive found that when he was sitting in a restaurant and felt cold because the heating was not turned up high enough, he felt obliged to endure the chill and say nothing. However, when his wife complained of being cold, he immediately asked the waiter to adjust it — for her.

A young mother shopped for groceries that would fit the likes and dislikes of every individual in the family — except herself. It simply didn't occur to her to consider what she might like or dislike.

You can ignore your own inner voice to such an extent that eventually your mood is determined not by what your own signal-giver wants and decides to feel, but by what other people do and say. Very likely your mood is this moment being determined by your son or daughter, in the sense that:

> If he or she is 'good', happy, or is succeeding at school you feel fine.

> If he or she misbehaves, or is unhappy or fails, you feel miserable.

If this is the case, your mood is being determined by a person outside yourself. It is as though you've taken the power to run your own feelings, your own life, which originally is *your* power, and given it to your adolescent. Now he or she determines your mood and all you can do is feel helpless and perhaps resentful about the way your son or daughter is using this power.

We believe that every time you look outside yourself for direction in this way and ignore your own inner signal-giver, you are betraying yourself. If you could be really sensitive to your inner voice, you could hear it crying out with hurt every time you do it. Ideally this inner being has a champion – namely, you – and when you fail to listen to it, it is as though its champion had abandoned it. It is when this has happened that feelings of depression, resentment, frustration arise. People almost always *experience* these uncomfortable feelings as having to do with events in the outside world, such as the misbehaviour of their children.

I'm depressed because of the way my son is turning out.

I'm frustrated because she just won't go to school.

We believe that in a deeper sense, however, these feelings are always 'caused' by a person's betrayal of his or her own signal-giver, which feels more and more desperate and smothered the more its signals are ignored.

It is important, for the work in the rest of the book, to get back in touch with this inner signal-giver, to commit yourself to take care of it and be loyal to it, and give it its rightful place as authority over your behaviour. We urge you to get into the habit of taking care of your own wants and needs.

In this chapter we give several specific exercises aimed at helping you learn to pay attention to your inner voice. The first four should be done the first time you read this chapter. The remaining three are to be done when you settle down seriously to prepare yourself to stand up for your own rights.

Exercise One

Think of all the people you are responsible for taking care of. Now, before reading further, count them on your fingers.

When you have counted all you can think of, stop, and ask

yourself this question: Did I include myself in this list?

Many of the parents we see put a great deal of energy into taking care of people, and readily spread their caring anywhere in the world – except towards themselves. Do you see what a put-down that is for one's own inner being?

Exercise Two

To make sure you have yourself firmly on the list of people you are responsible for taking care of, imagine that you suddenly discover you have one more child, a child you have been paying little attention to. This child is your own inner being. Now ask yourself whether you have been giving this child as much of your time, care and attention as you have the other persons you care about. Is there a sense in which you've been like the stepmother in the fairy tale, treating your inner child as a Cinderella, and favouring other people in the way the stepmother favoured the stepsisters?

Resolve that whatever else you may do in your life, from now on you will take care of your own inner being.

Exercise Three

Sit down with paper and pencil and before reading beyond this sentence, write down your answer to this question: 'What do I owe my child?' (Read no further until you have completed your answer.)

Now write down your answer to the question: 'What does my child owe me?'

When both questions are answered, compare the two answers. Did you make it a two-way street, so that you and your child owe each other approximately even deals? Or was it lopsided? If it was, do you know any reason why it 'should' be?

Now try out this idea just to see how it suits you: 'I don't owe my child anything. My child doesn't owe me anything. Each of us is a free person, able to run his or her own life – and free to do for the other what we *want* to do.'

Try out this idea too, to see how it suits you: 'I do not owe myself to anyone else. I owe myself to me.'

Exercise Four

Try out these sentences to see how they feel when you say them:

I have a right to privacy.

I have a right to be treated with courtesy.

I have a right to be happy.

I have a right to do as I wish with my own time.

Now ask yourself: 'Who is responsible for seeing that I have these rights?'

Try out this sentence: 'I owe my inner being these rights.'

It's possible that you may be finding these ideas startling, even shocking. Parents sometimes exclaim to us, 'Isn't it selfish to take care of myself? Immoral? Other people will disapprove of me and I will feel guilty.' Here are some of the ways in which we answer these questions.

We are *not* recommending that you become selfish and ride roughshod over other people. We do ask that you give your inner being equal rights with the other people in your life, and that you trust that, far from harming others, your doing so will actually be beneficial to them, too. Shakespeare put it well:

> This above all: to thine own self be true,
> And it must follow, as the night the day,
> Thou canst not be false to any man.

You can give to others only if you first have something to give. If you were surrounded by a thousand people all dying of thirst, and you had an empty bucket, you could do nothing for them until you filled your bucket. Learning to be loyal to and take care of your own inner being is filling your bucket. When you have done that, you can then take better care of others than ever before. This is because you will be giving to them because and if you want to rather than because you 'should' and this kind of help-because-I-want-to is far more meaningful than merely dutiful giving.

You may have the very good ambition to be a channel through which energy can flow for the good of others. If so, remember that

94

the energy can flow only if your channel is open and unblocked. Being on good terms with your inner being, taking care of it and accepting its guidance, is opening the channel.

We believe that basically what makes human beings happy is loving, cooperative relationships, giving freely and seeing others happy. If really set free, your signal-giver will lead you towards this. Thus, you do not have to be afraid it will lead you to selfish, destructive acts. Trust it and it will be trustworthy.

And finally, your taking care of yourself is good not only for you, but also for your child. We have been impressed again and again with how, when people learn to take better care of themselves, the benefits spill over onto the other important people in their lives as well. If your teenager is doing things that are on your particular parent's-life pile, he or she is probably seeing you not as a real, alive person, but as a kind of shadow, a convenience, a thing. Your teenager may be regarding you in somewhat the same way he or she would regard a petrol pump, something to go to for supplies but which has no feeling, deserves no consideration nor even a thank you, and is merely something to be used. It is not good for a person to grow up with this view of another person. If you begin taking your own inner signals seriously, your adolescent, too, will benefit by becoming more aware of you as a real person and learning how to treat people in order to get along in life.

Your teenager may be doing everything he or she can to get you to stand up for yourself, because every young person needs a definite, real person to interact with and come up against. By 'definite, real person' we mean a person who takes responsibility for getting his or her own needs met, and who does whatever he or she does because he or she wants to. For most children, the people who can best be this for them are their parents. Even a therapist cannot give this to a child the way a parent can.

In short, what has been missing for your teenager may well have been the part of you that wants, decides, feels for itself and takes care of itself. Thus we strongly urge: Put yourself, your wants, needs and feelings, back into the picture.

Let's begin working on this right now.

The first thing we ask you to do is learn to think and speak in the language of your inner being; that is to say, in *positive I-statements*.

Daring thoughts are constantly welling up inside you just as water wells up from a spring. They originate as I-thoughts:

I want a sandwich.

I itch.

I like that picture.

I feel tired.

I'm going to wash the car.

These are real, decisive, definite communications from you to yourself. They start out ever hopeful that you will hear them and do something about them, but very often they hit a barrier before that can happen. The barrier is made up of a set of fearful ideas like these: if I take care of this original impulse by speaking or acting it out:

People won't like me.

It will hurt people's feelings.

It will be selfish.

I will react too emotionally.

It will be impolite.

And so on.

The thoughts cannot get through this barrier intact; they can get through only in a weakened, distorted form. They are changed into *questions*, into *you* or *we* or *it statements*, into *negatives*.

Thus, if you are riding along in the country with a friend and the thought, 'I want a sandwich' comes up, it's likely to hit the barrier, 'To express this thought would be impolite or sound selfish,' and to come out as, 'When should we stop for a bite?' or 'Wouldn't you like to stop for something to eat?' Similarly:

I'm sleepy	can become	Why don't we go to bed?
I feel hurt and unfairly treated	can become	You're no good!
I'm happy	can become	How do you feel?
I want some peace and quiet this summer	can become	Son, why don't you find a job for the summer?

Thus, when the thoughts come out, they're no longer decisive. Notice how each one pushes some kind of responsibility onto whoever it's addressed to. We think that's why they often arouse antagonism in the other person, because actually they foist the decision making upon that person.

Two people who both have this barrier habit of thinking can

actually end up doing something neither of them wants.

Would you like to go to the cinema?

I don't know. How about you?

I thought maybe you'd like to go.

Well, what would you like to see?

I don't know; what would you like?

I don't think you'd like what's on at the Odeon.

Maybe you'd like the one at the Regal.

And so on.

We urge you to get back to the original thoughts, the direct, positive I-statements.

We do understand that there are barriers. You may shudder at the idea of speaking I-statements, thinking to yourself, 'It will hurt other people's feelings', or 'People won't like me.' These barrier thoughts are strong, and neither of the writers of this book has completely overcome them to this day. Because we've dealt with them for so long, though, we can also tell you some things about them.

> These barrier thoughts are very much exaggerated. The fears they inspire are far out of proportion to what is likely actually to happen when you begin to use I-sentences.

> The consequences you fear are more likely to come about, not when you use I-sentences, but when you talk in you's.

> Within a short time most people experience positive rather than negative effects – improved relationships with others and a sense of exhilaration – after they begin using I's.

> When unpleasant results do follow I-sentences, they are usually small and transitory.

> The longer term effect of I-sentences on your relationships with others is usually positive.

The next exercise, then, has to do with I-sentences.

Exercise Five

Right now, make some I-thoughts. Complete each of the following sentences in three different ways, and try thinking them, just to see what it feels like:

> I feel ... (excited, discouraged, hopeful, tired, puzzled, hungry, annoyed, an itch, etc.).

> I want ... (to go sailing, a better car, to feel happy, to have more friends, etc.).

> I'm going to ... (try out some of your 'wants' here just to see how it feels ... or fill in something else, such as: take care of myself, go to bed, read for a while, join the keep fit club ...)

In completing these, let yourself make up some answers without worrying about whether they are 'true' or not; consider the exercise as play and try out all kinds of sentences, simply to exercise your inner voice.

Take as an assignment that every day for the next week you will make up and speak at least three sentences of the form:

> I feel ...
>
> I like ...
>
> I want ...
>   or
> I am going to ...

Leave 'you' and 'we' out of these sentences until you are completely comfortable using 'I'.

A note of caution – a sentence with 'you' in it can be a you-sentence even if 'I feel' or 'I want' is part of the sentence. For example, 'I feel that you did it on purpose' and 'I want you to do it right away' are you-sentences whereas 'I feel upset when you use my things' is an I-sentence. Consider a sentence to be a finger. If the finger points back toward you, it is an I-sentence; if it points at someone else, it is a you-sentence.

To speed your learning to think in positive I-statements, simultaneously learn to drop certain other ways of thinking and speaking. There are some verbal expressions that serve to *prevent* you from taking care of yourself. You can learn to substitute other, more honest and effective habits for them.

Exercise Six

Take one of the following speech patterns every day, begin to notice how often you use it, and develop the habit of substituting a different expression for it.

● **Have to**
● **Should**

These expressions imply that *you* are not initiating anything, but are acting only because some outer force decrees you must. Every time you are tempted to use one of these, substitute the words *want to*, and see how this feels for you.

Instead of:	Try:
I have to get to work by nine.	I want to get to work by nine.
I should make that phone call.	I want to make that phone call.
I have to do that errand.	I want to do that errand.
I should pay those bills.	I want to pay those bills.

● **Negatives** (not, doesn't, can't, won't, isn't, etc.)

A negative tells the listener about something that does not exist, and therefore emphasizes the reverse side of what you actually mean. Whenever you're tempted to use a negative statement, imagine that you've just been stranded on a desert island and a helicopter pilot, making only one pass overhead, has called out to ask you what you want him to drop you in the way of supplies. It would be best to tell him what you *do* want; if you give him negatives (I *don't* want perfume; I *don't* want evening clothes; I *don't* want chocolates) you may starve.

In other words, drop the negatives from your language until you can talk comfortably using only positives.

● **Questions**

These, again, simply press your listener to take responsibility for a feeling or idea that originally belonged to you. Change them to positive statements.

Instead of:	Try:
Where were you?	I've been worrying about you, as I was expecting you home at five.
Where would you like to eat?	I'd like to eat at an Italian place tonight.

● **You, we, it**

We understand you could hardly use the language without some of these speech forms. However, to sharpen your idea of how you're actually using them, consider spending a day or two without saying these words except after 'if' or 'when' and only sparingly even then.

It's paradoxical, but in asking you to work so carefully on your speech patterns, we're actually wanting to help you become more spontaneous, more responsive to your original, inner impulse. In the seventh exercise we ask you directly to become more spontaneous.

Exercise Seven

'Purposely' do some small 'spontaneous' things. Resolve to do at least three small, non-duty, fun things every day. Let them come from you, on the spur of the moment. They need last only two or three minutes if you like.

Instead of doing the dishes right away, first go and sit in the garden for a few minutes.

Going out to the car, pick up a pebble and see if you can hit a tree trunk with it.

In the middle of making breakfast, try a new idea: some raisins might be nice in the orange juice.

If you set yourself to hear them, you may begin to notice all sorts of small, exciting urges from your signal-giver. These are the daring thoughts which in the past you might have squashed.

The above exercises are meant to give you a preliminary sense of what we mean by listening to your own signal-giver. You may have noticed, for example, that you cannot sincerely complete the sentence, 'I like...' without first doing a little mental survey of yourself, your situation, what you feel like, to see what you do like. This mental survey is what we mean by consulting yourself; we urge you to get into the habit of consulting yourself regularly and as a matter of course. Every once in a while, throughout your day, take a survey to see what your signals are saying, and allow yourself the thought, 'I feel such and such; I'm going to . . .' and so on.

Now we are coming to perhaps the most difficult idea in this book. It may be hard enough for you to learn to consult your signal-giver when things are going reasonably well in your life. It is important to learn to consult it also *when things go wrong*.

Are you aware of having feelings of worry, dread, anger, and so on now and then during the day? They're likely to come to you in terms of thoughts like this:

I hate this.

Ugh.

Oh, not again.

These experiences are signals from your inner being; it's trying to say to you, 'I'm hurting. Help me!' We think it is very important what you do when such feelings hit you.

You may have got into a habit that goes like this:

1. You're going along in your life, and something happens that's negative for you.

You realize you have a headache.

You remember that you will have to cope with your child when you get home.

You realize you've been cheated somehow.

Someone snubs you.

2. You find out that this is negative for you when your signal-giver tells you about it by giving you a painful 'twinge' which says, 'I'm hurting!'

3. Quick as a flash, you turn your attention away from your signal giver to something in the outside world, and begin struggling with that something. You think (or say):

Why is this happening?

This is terrible.

You are a no-good; you shouldn't do that; stop it.

I'm sunk and it's hopeless.

4. All too often, things get worse.

101

'I hate being everybody's slave.'

Thus, although you received a clear message from your signal-giver ('I'm hurting'), you switched your attention away from taking care of it and focussed instead upon something else which you felt was causing your unpleasant feeling – the weather, your child, the painfulness of your headache, the person who snubbed you. You began using your energy to work out why that something else behaved that way, what that something's behaviour means about what you must be, how to stop or get back at or change or placate that something. Notice that all of these thoughts set you up as done-to by something outside yourself. More important, they are *irrelevant* to what you really want. You're hurting, and you want to feel better, and yet not one of these thoughts or remarks will get that for you. Rather, they seem to make the situation even worse.

We think that in switching your attention away from taking care of the hurt your signal-giver described, you deserted that signal-giver. You are like a captain whose ship hits a rock, and who then begins to focus on the rock – working out how it got there, whether it is ice or granite and what this means about his ability as a captain. He'd be a better seaman and have a better chance of surviving if he focussed instead on doing something to take care of his endangered ship. In the same way we think you'd be doing a better job if, when you get a 'twinge', you focus on *taking care of your own being which hurts* instead of shifting your attention to some outside event. Keeping your attention on your own inner being, you could consult it about what would make it feel better and how you might take care of it. It has announced that it is hurting. Act as you might towards a dear friend who told you he or she was hurting, and ask it: 'What can I do for you? What will make this hurting better and get you into a happier situation? What do you really want and how can I go about getting it for you?'

So the new habit can go like this:

1. Something happens that's negative for you.

Someone snubs you.

2. Your signal-giver tells you about it by giving you a 'twinge' of pain, of anxiety.

3. You keep your attention focussed on that signal-giver and consult it as to what it wants you to do to make it feel better.

What do I want to do right away?

4. Then you wait a moment, keeping your attention focussed not on the disturbing event (the person who snubbed you) but on whatever inside you tells you what you like and don't like. If you're in pretty good touch with it, ideas about what things to do will begin to come to you. They may or may not have to do with the thing that disturbed you.

Actually, I'm hot and I want to go and have a shower.

I want a good relationship with this person who snubbed me, and I'm curious as to why he's upset. I'll tell him that.

I want to be away from this person. Therefore I'll leave the room.

I feel hurt and eating out will make me feel taken care of. Therefore I'm going.

The great advantage of waiting to act until you get the message from your inner being is that now, whatever you do, you will be doing it because you choose to and want to, rather than because you are acted upon automatically, like a robot.

The first few times you do this, you may receive and act upon answers that result in more discomfort for you in some way, rather than making you feel better. If this happens, you know that you have not listened well enough to your inner signal-giver. It knows what you most deeply want, and it will give you signals of discomfort about any answer that is wrong for you. You need only become more aware of it and commit yourself more deeply to being loyal to it.

Your son calls you a bad name. You consult your signal-giver about what would

103

make you feel better, and the first answer you get is, 'Hit him,' or 'Slap him!' You hit your son — and then you feel worse rather than better; you've won the current battle but you feel guilty and discouraged about the total situation. Now, looking back at the answer, 'Hit him,' you realize that a nagging feeling of 'not quite right' accompanied it; you were not completely relaxed and sure about it.

Here the best thing would be to wait for further answers. Don't worry about doing nothing at all about the situation until you get a clear message from yourself. Feel self-confident and wait for an answer that feels good when you are in a relaxed mood.

What if no answers come? Sometimes parents are quite out of the practice of hearing their inner voices, and say to us, 'I don't *know* what I want to do.' 'No answer comes!' If this happens, we suggest that you *prime* your signal-giver so that it can begin giving you answers. Purposely think of all the possible ways you might behave and present them all to your inner being, letting it approve or disapprove each choice. Think of dozens of choices for it.

What about telling this person off?

What about ignoring him or her?

What about getting yourself a drink?

Do you want to go roller skating?

What about going over and giving this person a hug?

What about fighting back?

What about phoning a friend and talking about skiing?

What about calling the police?

What about leaving right now and spending the night in a hotel?

What about going to do my favourite activity?

And so on.

Your signal giver will deliver a precise degree of approval or disapproval for each choice and you can then take the one with the highest approval.

Our overall point is this: that you may have been letting your inner being down in the bad times by ignoring it, failing to take care of it, and finally doing things that get you results you do not really want. We urge you to redirect your loyalty. Promise yourself that *every time you feel a 'twinge' you will keep your head and do your best to get for your inner being what it most truly wants.*

Some of the unpleasant events you experience are things over which you have little influence, such as the weather. Others you can change, or at least reduce the chance of their happening in the future. For these we will describe, in subsequent chapters, some specific ways of acting which can be instrumental in getting you what you want when these negative things happen to you. However, whether you can change the distressing outside event or not, taking care of your own inner voice, as we have been urging in this chapter, is vital.

The most important single thing you can do for yourself and for your teenager is to take hold of your own life and make it what you want and do what you truly want with it. Commit yourself to be loyal to and take care of your inner being.

Chapter Seven

Preparing to stand up for yourself

We're beginning work now on the items on the rest of your list – the troubling things your son or daughter does which do have an effect on your life. We will assume that you have gone carefully through the earlier part of this book and have already backed away from trying to control your child's life in areas that affect only him or her, if you ever were – so that what's left are items like the following which do seem to have an effect on your life:

Won't do chores.

Uses foul language around the house; calls me names.

Leaves a mess in the house.

Uses my clothes, hairdryer, transistor radio, without asking; gives them to friends.

Steals my money, drink, jewellery.

Doesn't clean up her dog's mess.

Runs up long distance phone bills.

Grows pot in the house; stores it in his room.

Knocks holes in the walls when he gets angry.

Uses my tools and leaves them out in the rain.

Wrecked my car.

Demands money.

Has friends, parties, in the house while we are at work.

Sponges; will neither go to school nor work.

Is damaging my relationship with my partner.

Some of these are things that lead a social worker to say to the parent, in real amazement, 'Why in the world do you put up with it?' and sometimes to go further and recommend, 'Don't put up with it!' However, the parent usually *doesn't know how* to stop putting up with it. This is what we want to show you.

We think that these parent's-life items get to you not because of what they are in themselves. You'd probably gladly do the work, undergo the pain, provide the things, clean up the mess, if doing these things were part of effective child rearing and you got the satisfaction of doing a good job and having a good relationship out of it. We think they get to you because of what they mean. When your teenager does these things, it's as though he or she were saying:

I don't care about you.

You're not a valuable person.

I don't have to pay attention to you.

You don't matter.

They hurt, then, because of the way they define you and your son or daughter. They say that he or she is irresponsible and inconsiderate and that you are merely a convenience or a shadow whose rights need not be considered.

If things like the above items are happening to you, we believe there's a sense in which you have allowed yourself to be taken too much as a convenience. You are being too much a doormat, a pushover.

Being a doormat is largely a matter of *your* attitude.

To get you out of this trouble with your teenager, we propose to teach you to stand up and leave the doormat attitude behind forever.

There are two general things to learn in order to do this. One is some specific techniques of assertiveness, which we will coach you on in Chapters 8 to 10. The other is an attitude – an attitude of feeling comfortable, relaxed, loving towards your teenager because you know you will take care of yourself and therefore your happiness is not at risk in the situation. In this chapter we will review ways of acting or thinking which we think contribute to such an attitude. You may or may not want to accept all of these ideas as right for you, but we do ask that you study them enough so that you understand them. We think the attitude they reflect is basic to your success in resolving the problems with your teenager and in becoming as happy as you'd like in your own life.

We've touched on all of these ideas in earlier parts of this book, so they won't be entirely new to you. Consider them now, one by one, as a check-up to put yourself into an appropriate frame of mind before tackling the assertive assignments of the next three chapters.

Keep Your Goals in Mind

When you're feeling pressed about something that's happening between you and your teenager, remember what your basic goal is. You want:

> To be happier yourself.

> To see your son or daughter being a responsible and decent person.

Hold on to this idea so that you do not let yourself be drawn into the irrelevant emotions we talked about in Chapter 7.

What most people most deeply want is happiness and fair, cooperative relationships with others. We believe that both you and your youngster do too. However, under stress or threat, people tend to forget all about what they are truly after and begin to operate as if their deepest concerns were:

> Who's going to win.

> Proving I'm right.

> Showing I can control my child.

> Proving that I am a good parent.

> What other people will think.

> What society says things should be like.

What the law says I must do.

We've not heard a parent say that what he or she most deeply wanted was one of these things, but we've seen a lot of parents act as if it were. That's very human behaviour, but in the long run it perpetuates the very problem the parent is struggling to change. We ask you to keep your head in the sense of keeping your perspective and remembering what you are really after even through stressful times and setbacks.

In moments of stress, reassure yourself by remembering that what you're after is a happier situation for yourself and a responsible and decent child.

Hold a Positive View of Your Teenager

Look at your kid's misbehaviour in a different way. You may have been believing that your teenager does troublesome things simply because he or she wants to, or is basically lazy, dishonest, careless, immature or dislikes you. In Chapter 3 we asked you to begin looking at them in a different way. Look at them as things your child does in order to keep him or herself defined as lazy, dishonest, and so forth, because he or she is afraid of standing up as a solid, responsible, good person, and these things enable him or her to play the irresponsible role. Consider them as precisely designed to get you to reinforce this definition by getting helplessly angry, feeling hurt, trying to force your adolescent to stop it, seeing him or her as a bad person and yourself as a bad, helpless parent. We ask that rather than continuing to function in this role for your son or daughter, you do something different.

Believe that your kid already is basically a solid, responsible, good person, and that he or she, like everyone else, basically wants a fair, loving, cooperative relationship with the people in his or her life. When you confront your son or daughter, speak to the basic part of him or her that wants this.

Your Attitude — It Can Actually Change Things

The way you *see* the situation between you and your teenager *influences* it. The attitude you take not only helps you decide how to act, but even more striking, your attitude influences his or her attitude and actions.

Attitudes are highly contagious. The attitude you're in when you relate with another person will powerfully influence the other to see things within the same general framework. Try it – look straight into the eyes of the next person you meet and give either a warm smile or a scowl, and notice its immediate impact on the other.

This influence is especially important in the parent-child relationship, simply because you are the parent, and your teenager is geared to expect authority and expertise from elders, despite what he or she may say or imply to the contrary. Thus your attitude can influence your teenager more than his or her attitude influences yours. Take responsibility for setting the mood and the atmosphere between you and don't let yourself get pulled into a contest, a who's-going-to-win attitude, even if that's what your teenager is doing.

Recognize that simply holding a positive attitude about your teenager will influence the problem you're having with him or her in a positive way.

An Equal Relationship

Consider what a relationship of equality between you and your son or daughter would be like. If you're having trouble, a basic problem is likely to be that your relationship with your son or daughter has shifted from one of equality to one in which one (or both) of you is trying to control the other – towards, in other words, a master-slave relationship. In the first half of this book we asked you to reverse any tendency towards your being the master, the child the slave. It will be equally important now to reverse any tendency towards you being the slave, the child the master.

You can reverse a you-slave, child-master tendency by taking your wants and rights as seriously as you do anyone else's, including your son's or daughter's, and standing up for them with all the passion that you would for any exploited being.

You began working on this in Chapter 6 and should go further with it now.

Examine your own ideas about the relationship and see whether any of the following are among them:

I'm obliged to support and care for my teenage child. He or she is under no obligation to me.

I'm responsible for him or her. He or she is not responsible for me.

My adolescent has a right to be supported and cared for by me without making any return. I have no particular rights in the situation.

We've heard many parents and teenagers express variations of this one-way view. Parents say things like:

I'm obliged to. I owe it to her to take care of her.

I have to put up with it; he's my son.

I'll start living my own life when they go off on their own.

Teenagers say things which mirror the same ideas, ideas that their parents are obliged to put up with them and to take anything that they do until they reach a certain age. A conversation one of us had with a fifteen-year old boy recently exemplifies this view:

'Who does the cooking around here?'
'Mum.'
'What about cleaning the place up?'
'Mum.'
'Rubbish?'
'Mum puts it in the garage and Dad puts it out on Wednes-days when he goes to work.'
'How about the back garden?'
'Dad likes to potter around out there at weekends.'
'Who changes the sheets and makes the beds?'
'Mum.'
'All of them?'
'Yes.'
'Why?'
(Shrug) 'That's her job.'
'What's yours?'
(Shrug) 'Nothing really. But Mum doesn't work so taking care of us is her job.'

Here are three further actual examples we have observed.

Colin (13) had just made a shambles of his father's workshop and another mess in the kitchen making himself a snack. His father asked him to clean things up, but Colin simply got on his motorbike for his usual late night at the pub. When his father said, 'Well, I'm not going to let you in until things are cleaned up.' Colin laughed and said, 'You have to; it's your duty.'

Ann (14) had friends in the house to smoke pot during school hours, while her mother was at work. She stayed out as late as she pleased at night, failed to clean up after herself in the house, and refused to do chores. Asked why her mother put up with all this and continued to support her, she said simply, 'She has to.'

Jeff (17) had just wrecked his mother's car and left it some miles away on the motorway. He had not done any housework nor contributed to the family for many months. When his mother expressed her utter frustration, he leaned back in his armchair and said in mock comfort, 'Well, only one more year, mother dear!'

Youngsters with this view of their parents tend not to feel grateful for what those parents do for them; rather, they may be resentful because their 'servants' are not doing more. We've talked with teenagers who honestly felt cheated because their parents didn't provide them with cars, or because the ones they were given were not good enough. Obviously, these teenagers feel that it is their right to be supported and taken care of, given to, without making any return. Then they feel abused and angry when their parents' offerings do not meet their expectations.

If any of this fits the way things have been going between you and your son or daughter, then we think it's time for you to make a Declaration of Human Rights for yourself, and resolve to uphold it. Consider substituting for the above attitudes, ideas like:

My child and I have equal rights as human beings.

My child is responsible for taking care of his or her own wants and happiness, and I am responsible for mine.

My first task is to be loyal to my own inner being; doing that will actually be helpful to those around me.

The best parent is neither a slave nor a master, but an equal human being.

The best thing I can give my boy or girl is a model that it is all right to take care of one's own feelings, wants, and ideas, and to be happy.

To summarise this idea of equality, then, consider moving towards a relationship of equality between you and your teenager.

113

Your Rights

If you have decided you do want a more equal relationship with your son or daughter, decide now what your rights are, and commit yourself to stand up for them.

How can you tell what your rights are?

At first, it may seem to you that your rights are something you inherently have, as much a part of you and as unchangeable as your ears and hands. However, when you realize that people have very different 'rights' in different times and different parts of the world, you begin to see that there is no such thing as an inherent right.

Your 'rights' are what you and the people in your life believe or agree they are. For example, if you and the government believe or agree that you have the right to own property, then you do. If there is no such belief or agreement, then you don't. *And if you are not satisfied with the rights you have in any current situation, it's up to you to pick out and claim new rights for yourself that you think would be more fair.* It's always been this way with rights between people. For example, in olden days the 'right to vote' simply did not exist; there was no such thing. Then people invented this right, claimed it and struggled for it, and from then on the 'right to vote' did exist. At first, though, men had this right and women didn't, and during the time covered by this decision, that was 'right' – because people in general agreed that it was. Then women claimed this right and struggled to establish it for themselves, and now it's generally agreed that they do have it.

In other words, your rights do not exist anywhere in any absolute sense; it's up to you to make them up and claim them.

When you do decide you want some rights you have not been accorded lately, prepare yourself to stand up for them. (We will show you how in the next chapters.) This standing up is necessary because if other people have been catered to for some time they tend to think they should be catered for, that this is their right, and they will object when you suggest something different. If your teenager has been walking all over you for some time, he or she may well assume this is the way things *should* be, and will defend it. In a sense, by not claiming your right to equality, you have let your son or daughter believe you don't have that right, and now he or she is used to this. Therefore, when you first claim new rights, you will probably have to retrain your adolescent to accept them. It's as though a gardener's son and a prince had been playing chess over the years, and the gardener's son has always held back so that the prince could win. After some time both are likely to assume that the prince has the right to win and the gardener's son doesn't – simply because it's always been that way. If the gardener's son now wants to re-establish his 'right' to a fair win, he'll have some re-training to do, and the prince may very well object, feel unfairly treated and resentful.

We've noticed that adolescents act very much like princes when previously humble parents begin to stand up. Consider the following true story of an eighteen year old boy who actually threatened to run away because his father would not buy him a (third) new car.

A well-to-do father provided cars for all of his children when they reached seventeen. The fourth child wrecked his new car, so the father provided another. When this one was also wrecked, the father declined to provide a third. The boy now felt genuinely resentful and unfairly treated! He had become used to the idea that Dad provides cars, and he felt Dad had no right to withhold one.

Now, we think that if your teenager has been doing the kinds of things we're talking about in this chapter, it's very likely that you have been accorded fewer rights than you'd like and than you think is fair. We'd like to see you decide upon some new, more fair rights for yourself and then commit yourself utterly to taking care of them. Be ready to work to establish a new view of the fairness of your rights in relation to your teenager, just as the voters, the gardener's son, and the father had to do in the above examples. You will have to provide a new definition of your rights, and stand up for them.

Here are some sample rights other parents have decided they want and will stand up for.

- *The right to privacy.*

- *The right to my own relationships with my spouse and friends.*

- *The right to be free of fear of violence.*

- *The right to feel secure about my belongings.*

- *The right to some time of my own.*

- *The right to be treated with courtesy.*

- *The right to relationships that are two-way rather than only one-way streets.*

- *The right to reasonable peace and quiet.*

- *The right to feel everyone is carrying his or her weight and I am not supporting a layabout.*

- *The right to lock up my house at night and know no one will come in after that.*

By the way, these 'rights' are not so very different from the things children say they want for themselves. Make sure you're granting your teenager rights equivalent to those you now want for yourself, so that you can have a truly equal relationship. It will not work to claim any of these basic rights for yourself while withholding it from your son or daughter.

How does the law fit in with this question of your rights? Many parents (and we did the same ourselves) think it is useless to consider what their rights are because they're 'legally responsible' for their children. They take this to mean that they're legally bound to support their children, make them behave properly, put up with whatever they do, without recourse, and pay for any damages they incur. Naturally, this makes them feel hopeless about claiming any rights for themselves.

The good news here is that, although indeed the law does state that you are responsible for your kid, it's much more reasonable than most parents realize, and it need not at all prevent you from claiming basic human rights in the relationship with your kid.

We know of no law anywhere that says you must put up with the kind of behaviour we're talking about in this chapter. Under the 1944 Education Act it is the duty of parents to ensure that their children are registered at a school and that they attend that school. If you deliver your child to the gates of the school and he or she later absconds you can't be prosecuted. If the child fails to attend school and this can be proved to be the result of parental negligence then a

116

court action can be taken against the parent by the local authority. The child, who, it is deemed, is not receiving adequate education, can be brought before the juvenile court which decides whether a care order should be taken out or not. If it is, then your child is removed from your care and placed in a local authority establishment whose legal charge he or she then becomes.

It's true that you can be assessed for damages your teenager might incur but there is likely to be a legal limit to your financial responsibility. In England, for example, that limit is £1,000 compensation or fine and under the Criminal Justice Act parents' ability to pay is taken into consideration. Parents can't be ordered to pay costs, damages or compensation, if they can show that they have not contributed to the wrong done by neglecting to exercise due care over the child. In cases of criminal damage parents of young persons over 17 years of age are not legally responsible for financial reparation and the young person could be given a prison sentence.

So there's no point in letting your behaviour be determined by fear of being ordered to pay compensation. And you can't control it anyway, whether you claim your rights or not. Letting yourself be walked all over by your teenager doesn't save you from the possibility of being sued, so you might as well claim your rights. Actually, we think that teenagers are less likely to act out and do damage when parents stand up for themselves.

In summary of this discussion of your rights, *decide right now what your rights are and commit yourself to stand up for them.*

Fear of Encounter

The next thing to do, after you've decided what your fair rights are and that you will stand up for them, is to begin coming to terms with your fears of the encounters you may have to undergo when you claim those rights.

Parents sometimes put up with a lot from their children because they dread the disapproving or disappointed or angry looks or the scene that might result if they stood up for themselves. This is quite natural. Nobody enjoys disharmony and the really terrible position of standing out all alone against opposition. One of us very well remembers the experience of this fear, over and over again, in situations like this:

I had told our kids I wanted no raids on the fridge in the hour before dinnertime. I was sitting in the living room at about 5.30 when I heard our son, 16, come into the kitchen and open the refrigerator. I knew the next step I wanted to take was to give him an I-sentence reminder: 'Son, I really don't want eating before dinnertime.' I was so afraid to say it that I began literally to shake. The temptation was almost overwhelming to pretend that I had not heard him and therefore would not have to say it.

This fear of encounter is of course justified in one sense. It's true that you may indeed get some sour looks or scenes as you begin to stand up for yourself, especially if you've been walked over for some time. Even though he or she very much needs the limits you will set, no young person of any spirit is going simply to accept them and say, 'Thanks.' It's part of the game to fight back for what the adolescent thinks are his or her rights. And adolescents can do all sorts of things to pressure you into backing down once you've begun to stand up. They can say things like:

You don't care about me.

I hate you.

I'll run away.

I wish I (or you) were dead.

They can give you the silent treatment, or the gloomy, I'm-so-mistreated treatment. They can have tantrums and break things.

Linda (15) had been getting out of doing any jobs for some time. Her mother asked her to sweep the floor. Saying nothing, Linda walked out the door and ran away from home.

Anna (17) was in the habit of pestering her mother for the car every morning. Her mother would stall, make excuses and finally give in to her. One day her mother said 'No' whereupon Anna swept all the dishes off the breakfast table. When her mother stood firm in saying no, Anna seriously threatened to push her ailing grandmother into the swimming pool.

Carol (14) used to come home well after suppertime and then eat the leftovers in the kitchen, but she never cleaned up after herself. Her mother requested that she do so and stuck to the request, upon which Carol threw a tantrum in which she broke many of the things in her room and screamed so loudly that the neighbours became alarmed and called the police.

Now, we know that the prospect of any of this kind of behaviour can be frightening. We also believe that the less afraid of them you are, the less likely they are to happen. That's because this is blackmailing behaviour – things the adolescent does to pressure you into giving in to him or her. No sensible young person is going to waste tantrums on someone who clearly is not impressed by them.

Further, there's a sense in which the fear of encounter is not justified. It's this. We think that what you're most deeply afraid of here is not what he or she will do. You could probably stand most of that very well if it weren't directed at you. What you actually most dread may be the idea of yourself standing out in everyone's view as a real, solid person who dares to hold up his or her head and say, 'I claim these rights for myself.' We well know that this can indeed be a nerve-racking thing. We also know that, far from being actually harmful or dangerous, standing out in this direct way is the very essence of good human communication.

If you've been dreading the encounters, it may well be because you feel helpless about them, do not know what to do during them. Having something definite to do will ease this fear. We'll be giving you that in the chapters that follow. So let yourself realize that you will have all the tools you need to handle encounters.

Realize, too, that in the encounter you are actually giving your son or daughter the most precious thing you can – a piece of yourself – and he or she very much needs some of yourself from you.

Also, if you're afraid of encounters in general, realize that this situation with your teenager is a chance for you to free yourself of that fear. You can learn to be comfortable with the scenes and even enjoy them – come to look forward to the feeling of exhilaration and accomplishment you get from knowing you can handle them.

An exercise: If you can, listen to some younger children talking together – children between say five and ten. Notice how outspoken they are – flagrant, forthright, bossy. They seem unafraid of encounter. As an adult, you have so much more life experience than these little ones; what would it be like if your little gems came tumbling out in this way? You and everyone else would know you're alive and maybe all of you would thrill to the encounter!

Thus, regarding encounters, you will have the tools to handle them and they can be exhilarating. After you have successfully dealt with a few of them, you will feel more at ease with them and will probably also notice that they become less frequent and less intense.

Being Open

In Chapter 6 we asked you to begin becoming more sensitive to what your own wants, discomforts and feelings are, and to use I-sentences talking about them. When you do this you are doing a number of things. You are being open; you are taking a first step in the direction of taking care of yourself; and you are giving something of yourself to the other person in direct communication. *You are also developing a habit that can be counted on to carry you through every interaction.* Whenever an uncomfortable feeling comes over you –

fear of the encounter, worry about the outcome, confusion over what to do or say next, or any uncomfortable feeling, you can begin to take care of yourself by focussing on your inner being, asking what it is experiencing, and then expressing that experience to whoever confronts you:

I can't think of anything to say. I just don't know what to say.

I feel absolutely helpless about this.

I'm so worried the house will burn down.

With every bit of genuine openness like this, spoken as I-sentences and without you's, you will find your power coming back to you and the situation progressing towards greater equality.

Realize that a major aspect of bringing about an equal relationship and resolving these parent's-life items is your own openness.

In summary, the attitude we are encouraging you to develop, as you work on the parent's-life items, involves these aspects:

Concentrate on remaining self-confident and remember that what you're after is your own happiness and a responsible young person who can make his or her own decisions.

Assume that your teenager is basically a solid, responsible person who is doing these troublesome things because he or she has little practice in standing out as a good and competent person and is afraid to do so.

Understand that by taking this attitude towards the situation you are already beginning to improve it.

Take as your goal an equal-human-beings relationship between you and your teenager.

Decide upon your fair rights in the relationship and resolve to stand up for them. Realize that if you can count on yourself to take care of your own rights, you can be relaxed and confident no matter how any specific interaction turns out.

Realize there may be some encounters, and expect that your hesitancy about them can change to confidence and even pleasant anticipation as you practise handling them.

Count on your own openness as a major tool in all of this.

Chapter Eight

Eliminating triggers and reinforcers

Now we are ready to begin working on the specific problems that may be left after you have sincerely worked through the first seven chapters of this book.

Please review and revise your list of parent's-life items at this point. That list may have shifted and changed and some items may even have disappeared when you handed responsibility for the kid's-life items over to your son or daughter. Prune the list down to things that are still problems for you, including things that have come up within the last week or two after you dropped efforts to control kid's-life items listed on pages 21, 107 to 108, and any aspects reserved from kid's-life items in Chapter 2.

Now let's begin working on that up-dated list.

As a first step, look for any obvious ways in which, unknowingly, you may actually have been *inviting* the behaviour on this list. Bear each item in mind as you read this chapter and consider carefully anything you may have been doing to make it more likely to happen.

Parents help bring about the very behaviour that bothers them in two ways: by *triggering* it before it starts, and by *reinforcing* it after it's been done. The trigger is usually some form of you-message or a question. The reinforcement is negative attention. That's why we encourage you, when you're coping with misbehaviour, to *make I-statements* instead of you-messages or questions, and to focus *positive, helping attention* on *yourself* instead of negative attention on your kid.

Let's go over some of the specific ways in which you may be triggering or reinforcing the very behaviour that is bothering you. We'll talk about five kinds of items that are especially likely to be encouraged by parents:

Lying.

Stealing.

Saying worrying or frightening things, name-calling, swearing.

Having a sullen or belligerent attitude.

Abusing favours a parent has granted.

Lying

If your child's lying has been one of your problems, you may be getting less of it now that you have handed him or her responsibility for the kid's-life items. That's because children sometimes lie when they must ask your permission for kid's-life items and think you may say No. If Marilyn, for instance, wants to go to the shopping centre with a friend who has recently been charged with shoplifting, it's tempting for her to say to you in a lie: 'Mum, may I go to Paula's? We're going to work on our school project.' According to the old way of doing things, you'd be likely to give your permission to this, and she could then go to the shops feeling righteously that she has successfully fooled the dictator. However, if you've given up the job of permitting or forbidding activities, as we asked you to in Chapters 2 to 4, your daughter cannot so easily justify lying, and is less likely to do it. According to the new way, if Marilyn still asks you permission for an innocent visit to her friend's house, you will say only, 'I'm glad you told me; I'll know to delay lunch,' or perhaps, 'I'm out of the permission-giving scene, but thanks for letting me know where you'll be.' You haven't picked up her lie; you've left her stuck with it. Marilyn will then have to go to the shops knowing that she has unnecessarily lied to you; there's no dictator to justify her lying for her. This is less comfortable for her than the old way, and there's more room for her to be straight with you instead and to say, 'Mum, I'm going to the shops with Susan' – without lies. There's more room for you, too, since you've given up forbidding her or granting permission, to express concern, interest, and trust. 'I feel uncomfortable about that because I worry that Susan might shoplift again and perhaps get you both into trouble. And yet I know you'll do what's right for you about going.'

Even if you've given your son or daughter responsibility for the kid's-life items, though, you may still be getting other lies, about all sorts of things. If so, look to see whether you are *triggering lies by asking questions*, and *reinforcing them by focussing negative attention on your teenager when he or she lies*.

Begin with the resolve to ask your boy or girl no questions whatsoever for at least a week.

This probably won't be as difficult as it sounds. Simply stay a little alert to the way you talk with your son or daughter, and every time you feel the impulse to ask a question, either say nothing at all, or change the question to something you can express as an I-statement.

Instead of:	Try this:
Have you done your jobs yet?	I'd like to know the bathroom is clean by now.
Why don't you say hello to me when I come home?	I feel left out when I don't get a hello.
	or
	I'd like a hello when I get home at night.
How are you getting home?	I worry about your safety and I'd like to know you'll be getting home safely.
Is your homework done?	Say Nothing! (A clear kid's-life item)

There's one kind of question we especially caution against – the question in which you test whether your son or daughter will lie by asking about something you already know. For example:

> The school telephoned home to ask whether Jennifer (14) was ill, since she had not come to school. That afternoon Jennifer's mother asked her, 'How was school today?'

We think this is entrapment. We recommend against it partly because it is likely to induce a lie from Jennifer and thus give her more practice at the very thing her mother doesn't want, and even more because asking this sort of question has the same elements of deceit and manipulation as the lying itself. A simple statement and an I-message would be more effective:

> The headmaster phoned today to ask why you weren't at

school. I hate to get phone calls from the school and would really appreciate freedom from that sort of call.

When you stop the questions, the lies are likely to decline dramatically. You may still get a few that your kid volunteers because he or she doesn't yet realize you're no longer going to play ball; for these, make sure that when you hear them, you do something different from giving your boy or girl negative attention. Any kind of worried or angry reaction will feed the lying habit, so instead do something like this:

Simply say 'Hm' and walk away to do your favourite thing.

Pretend you're listening to a neighbour's child telling you something in a friendly discussion in which, even if you privately think he or she is lying, there's no need to check it out, and you can simply be polite.

Say, 'I'm uncomfortable because I keep getting the feeling I'm being lied to, so I'd like to stop this conversation.'

If you make sure you've truly stopped questions and negative attention, we can't promise you'll get as good results as Kathy's mother did in the following true life experience. Yet we wouldn't be surprised either. The strategy is so often successful that we've come to feel that lying is one of the easiest problems for parents to deal with.

Mrs. R. complained that Kathy (8) lied almost continuously. She lied about her own activities ('I got an A in school today') and she also 'made up' tall tales about things she had seen and heard. Investigation showed that Mrs. R. asked questions almost continuously, all the way from, 'How are you?' and 'How was school?' to 'What are you doing now?', 'Why did you steal my make-up?', 'What are you going to do next?' and 'Don't you want to be good?' and 'Why do you lie?' She was taught to stop all questions, and instead either make I-statements or keep silent. In other words, she was to stop triggering Kathy's lies. She was also told to respond to any colourful tales with a genuine expression of interest, if she felt it: 'That's interesting!' In other words, she was to stop reinforcing Kathy's lies by giving them negative attention. She made a heroic turnabout, following our suggestions to the letter. Though we all expected a longer-term struggle with the lies, they stopped immediately.

Of course, when the lying stops you may also realize that what bothered you was not just the lying itself, but the thing the lying was *about*. If your lad is lying about going to school, or about sniffing glue, or about whether he has stolen your jewellery, it won't solve your problem if only the lying stops. You want the truancy, drug abuse, or stealing to stop. In such a case, congratulate yourself on being able to stop the lying! Then deal with the other, underlying problem directly. If it's a kid's-life item, re-read Chapters 2 to 4. If it's a parent's-life problem continue through this chapter and the next ones.

Stealing

Sometimes parents report things like this:

> I get paid in cash, and my son Tom (16) seeks it out wherever I put it and steals some of it.

> Sandra (14) takes my clothes and jewellery and sells them to her friends.

> David (16) brought two friends into the house while I was on a business trip and let them go through my cupboards. They found £45 grocery money I'd left for my wife, and they took it.

Parents often begin a two-step programme of reinforcing-and-triggering stealing right after the first theft occurs. They do it by (1) focussing negative attention on the person who stole, by scolding, asking questions, punishing – and by (2) proceeding to leave valuable things available to be taken the next time. The more the stealing worries them and the more they want to be able to trust their children, the more likely they are to do these things.

The basic thing they can do to resolve the stealing problem is

126

anything different from these two methods. Your job is to decide upon definite ways to act that will not give your teenager negative attention and will not invite him or her to steal again. There's room for all sorts of creative decisions about what to do instead, and any of them is likely to work even better if you pick it out yourself. That's because *what* you do is less important than that it be something you can do while feeling comfortable and relaxed, without emotional charge, and you know best what that would be. For example, you might use each theft as a signal to you to begin your favourite activity, announcing to all (including the probable thief) that you were doing so in order to ease the pain of the theft. Another possibility would be to give the stolen object to the thief.

In a story by Victor Hugo, a man stole some silver plates from a priest who had given him food and shelter. When, later, gendarmes brought him to the priest to check his claim that the treasures they found in his possession had been given to him, the priest announced that indeed they were a gift. This giving of the precious silver was a crucial turning point in the man's life, leading him to a much better way of living.

Again, the crucial feature of each solution is not the behaviour itself, but rather that you feel relaxed and unworried as you do it. If solutions like these above leave you feeling that you are not being taken care of, consider the following two straightforward and practical steps.

First, make sure you're not inviting the stealing by leaving desirable things around when you know there's a stealing problem in your house. Look at the kind of thing that's getting stolen; if you'd lock it up in a strange hotel room, do the same in your house. You won't leave purses or wallets, loose cash or jewellery, or even appealing little things like electronic watches and transistor radios lying about if you sincerely mean to keep them and you know stealing has been going on.

Tell your son or daughter in an I-message that you're going to make your things secure. For instance, 'Carol, I've noticed that some of my cash has disappeared, so I'm going to keep it elsewhere from now on.'

Many are the parents we have coached to do this.

Mary's mother was bringing up two children alone in cramped quarters; the only private place she allowed herself was a box on top of the wardrobe, where she kept jewellery, cigarettes and some change. Several times a week she would notice some of these things were missing, and she and Mary (13) would then have a row about it. The pattern of the rows was quite constant: Mother would ask whether Mary had taken something, Mary would deny, Mother accuse, Mary would get angry, Mother would cry. We taught Mary's mother to stop all questions, accusations and crying, and obtain a sturdy lock for her box.

There was a continual shadow over Roger (15) in his family. Father had a jar full of pennies in the cupboard, and every time the level seemed a little lower than it had been, both parents suspected Roger had taken some. He, of course, denied it. We recommended to the father that he lock up the pennies.

Making your things secure will probably not be enough to resolve the stealing problem for you. For one thing, if that's all you do, your teenager may take it as a game or a contest, and manage to seek out the hiding places, break the locks, prise open the drawers. For another, you probably don't want to lock things up in your own house until your son or daughter is old enough to leave home.

The second, more difficult, thing we ask you to do is to turn off any negative attention and substitute a cheerful taking care of yourself when you think you've been stolen from.

We have no doubt that youngsters steal because they are afraid to stand up and be defined as good, happy, responsible people, and stealing is an easy way to keep themselves safely defined as bad and irresponsible. They could acquire almost anything they steal in other ways, but those other ways would involve being straight-forward and perhaps industrious and would define them as being responsible. Stealing, on the other hand, proves they are no-good – and that's why they do it. The best way of combating the stealing, then, is to make sure it does not work – that is, that it does not brand him or her as bad, through negative attention – and to do what you can to enable him or her to become comfortable with feeling like a good and responsible person. *Telling* your adolescent that he or she is good won't do this, but you can do it by being a model, showing him or her that you yourself feel good, happy and responsible, that you will take care of yourself, and that you cannot be provoked into giving negative attention. With you as a model, the young person can then little by little take courage to feel good and responsible, and will no longer need the stealing to prove otherwise.

How do you cheerfully take care of yourself when your son or daughter has stolen from you? We ask you to do just the sort of thing you'd do if a part of the roof fell in – that is, take action to get it fixed, perhaps ask for help, and in any case, do not scold or blame your teenager at all. You are the one who's been injured by being robbed, and your job now is to do something to make it up to yourself. Here are a few examples to show how taking care of yourself might go. Notice that all avoid negative attention and emphasize, instead, I-messages and focus on getting fair treatment for yourself.

Suppose that you notice that money is missing from your purse or wallet. Of your two children, Ben has taken money before and you therefore suspect that he has done it this time too, although you are not sure. You say,

'Wendy and Ben, I've just noticed that there is £5 missing from my purse. I'd like help in getting it back.'

'I didn't take it.'

'Me neither.'

'I understand what you're saying, and I'm saying I want it back. If I don't get it back by tomorrow, we may be eating a lot of lentil soup next week, since that was part of the grocery money.'

The next step may be that you or someone else 'finds' the money. It mysteriously turns out to be in your purse after all, or Ben unexpectedly 'finds' it in the kitchen drawer where you usually keep your purse (we have had instances in which just this has happened). If the money shows up like this, accept it casually and resist sarcasm. If it does not, then serve a great deal of lentil soup until you've recovered the equivalent of your £5 for yourself.

With variations to fit the individual situation, we've trained many parents whose teenagers have been stealing from them to take care of themselves:

David (16) was a quiet, rather shy boy who very much wanted friends. One day his father came home from a business trip and found that £65 was missing from his cupboard. David gave him the following explanation. He had been very impressed by two older boys he met who talked rough and were obviously more sophisticated in the ways of the world than he. While his parents were out, he had invited these boys into the house and did not object when they went through his parents' bedroom. They found £65 in David's father's cupboard, and promptly disappeared with it. Upon hearing this, David's dad called the police; however, there turned out to be confusion about who and where the two boys were and exactly who had the money now. We coached the father to treat the matter just as he would if a friend had lost some of his (Dad's) money. There was neither scolding nor punishment of David; Dad simply told him that he considered David responsible for the house and everything in it while the parents were away, and that he expected the money to be replaced. David agreed to pay it from his after-school job. Dad also told David he wanted no strangers in the house when he wasn't there, and that if he had to, to feel comfortable while away, he would hire a caretaker, though he would much rather count on David to take care of him in this matter.

Tricia (15) and Marilyn (16) were two volatile and dramatic sisters who felt free to do whatever occurred to them to further their fun. They regularly helped themselves to their mother's possessions and seemed unmoved by her complaints, accusations, pleas, and even crying about it. One day she was especially disconcerted to see that an expensive sweater had disappeared from her wardrobe. This time she simply told her daughters firmly, 'I want my sweater back.' The girls of course *denied knowledge of the sweater; they shouted, became sullen, claimed unfair treatment. At one point one of them stormed furiously out of the house rather than answer her mother. Mother was able to stay fairly relaxed and comfortable through all this because she knew exactly what she would do no matter what the girls did, and because she focussed on what she was going to do rather than on her daughters. She simply stood firm and repeatedly made only one response to anything the girls said or did: 'I want my sweater back.' After several hours of this, she also told the girls, 'I want my sweater back, and if I don't get it by tonight I will definitely ransack your wardrobes and throw your clothes in the swimming pool.'* She was obviously prepared to do just this. Eventually Marilyn broke down and, weeping, said, 'Well, give me time. I lent your sweater to a friend, and I've just now got her on the phone. She'll bring it back in the morning.'*

Sally (13) had spent some time in care due to persistent stealing. The first day she was back at home, her mother's new hairdrier disappeared. Her mother was sure Sally had given or sold it to her friends, but had no hard evidence for this and knew Sally would deny it if confronted. We suggested that the mother announce to the family (which included three other girls) that she was upset by the loss of her hairdrier and that, in order to take care of herself, she would use the grocery money to buy another one, keeping enough money to buy plenty of bread but nothing else for the family. She was to explain that although she didn't at all like going on bread and water or putting the rest of the family on it, she preferred that to letting her inner being be injured without anything being done to take care of it.

Sally's mother didn't get her hairdrier back but she did experience a gratifying feeling of satisfaction and accomplishment in having, for almost the first time, stood up for herself. She also noticed that Sally's sisters, in addition to complaining about the unfairness of the situation, did have a lot to say to Sally about it. In the months that followed, Sally's mother persisted and, though the going was tough for a while, things eased up greatly for her.

We have been talking about what to do if your teenager steals from you. But stealing from brothers or sisters is another matter. If this happens, you will be strongly tempted to become the family judge again and settle the dispute, probably by scolding or punishing the miscreant. Don't. Empathize with the one who was stolen from if you wish, and say that you know he or she has what it takes to deal with the matter. You are helping the sibling more by giving this sort of message than by moving heaven and earth to get some belonging back for him or her. The wronged child will work out how to handle the situation if you stay out of it.

Saying worrying or frightening things, name calling, swearing.

Included in this category are such things as:

Saying I don't love him.

Calling me bad names.

Whenever we have a row, threatening to burn down the house.

Using foul language.

Saying she'll run away.

Saying she's going to kill herself.

Saying he'll blow our heads off tonight while we're asleep.

These are all things youngsters *say*. Generally, they say them to their parents for one of two reasons:

1. Because something is a real problem; the young person means what he or she says and wants help in dealing with it.
2. Because it gets a rise out of the parent.

If your son's or daughter's talk is for the first reason, it would be best for you to do something effective about it. If it's for the second, it would be best if you turn your attention elsewhere. In neither case would it be helpful for you to give negative attention by becoming upset, hitting, shouting back, or feeling worried, guilty, frustrated or angry about it.

Therefore, we recommend that the first time or two any of these

---

* More later on taking physical actions like this. They can rebound unless they're thought out ahead of time and you are utterly sincere and committed about them.

things is said, you take it seriously, express your concern and offer to help. Further, if what your child says seems to you to imply a real danger, do what you can to avert it – perhaps by notifying the police, or by taking your child to a doctor for referral to a psychiatrist. For example, the parents of the boy who said he would blow their heads off called in the police. We also asked them to remove the gun they had in the house. The parents whose son said he would burn the house down offered to find a sympathetic doctor if he wanted it, and they also called the police.

Then, once you've taken these reasonable precautions, if your teenager continues to say things like this without making an effort to solve the problem, we'd start considering him or her to be blackmailing: that is, using words to egg you into giving negative attention by getting upset or to get you to back down on some stand you have taken. Our basic recommendation: use the assertive techniques of the next chapters, but *first make sure you're not encouraging these remarks by the way you react to them.* Stop allowing yourself to become upset every time you hear something like this.

Often when we see a parent bothered by what a teenager is saying, it seems to us there's a bullfight going on and the parent is being the bull. We've often wished we could whisper a few words to bulls in real bullfights, in which the bull has the power and the matador controls it. He needs only flick a small red flag to make the bull become upset, roar, and come thundering at him in a charge. No doubt the bull believes that his problem is the matador, or at least the red flag; however, as we see it, his problem is his own readiness to get upset and charge every time the matador wants him to and gives him the signal to do so. We'd like to tell the bull:

Try not charging.

You're playing right into this person's ploys by getting angry everytime he waves a flag. Think of how foolish he would feel if he couldn't make you do it. He would suddenly be the one with a problem.

Your adrenalin is precious. Take care of it; hoard it; don't pour it out so recklessly in anger or worry at someone else's signal.

Please consider whether there is any way in which you've been overreacting to things your children say. Decide that whatever you do from now on when your boy or girl says things like this, you will not turn on your anger, worry, guilt, frustration, nor begin shouting, hitting, or crying, when he or she gives the signal. Don't be a bull.

We once observed a perfect example of a child being manipulated in this way by another child. Read it and ask if by any chance you have been reacting as Peter did in the following situation:

Carol (10) and Peter (9) had got into an argument of the, 'It is so!', 'It is not!', 'It is so!' variety. When they were well into it, Carol's responses gradually became shorter and shorter ('It is!' and then merely, 'Is!') while Peter, insisting that she shut up entirely, gave more and more furious and complicated answers ('It is not, you stupid!'). Soon he began hitting the walls and stamping the floor in helpless rage. In the end, Carol sat lazily on her bed and only needed to give the tiniest of squeaks in whatever timing she wished to send Peter into a frenzy of screams.

Clearly in this case the issue was no longer the particular thing the two children were arguing about, but rather one person's discovering how to get a rise out of another one. Peter apparently never realized that he was being turned on and off by someone else, and that his outbursts weren't getting him anything he wanted.

Jamie (9) and Bob (12) had their mother and their new, very earnest stepfather frantic. When pressed to say exactly what the boys did to achieve this, the parents could hardly define it, and finally pinned it down to things the boys said. It appeared that whenever either parent tried to set a limit (asking Jamie or Bob to help out, to go to bed, to make less noise, and so on) the boys would say, 'You can't make me', 'I don't like it here; I'm going to phone my father and get him to come and fetch me', or they would laugh. These things, especially the low, teasing laugh, drove the stepfather wild. He had worked himself into a state of nervous tension and, literally, high blood pressure after several months of this situation. It seemed clear that by taking what the boys said so seriously and by becoming so upset over it, he was encouraging their verbal teasing.

Among other things, we asked these parents to call the boys' bluff on all threats that they would phone their father ('You're welcome to use this phone to call your Dad, and meanwhile I want less noise around here.') We also asked them to hear what the boys said more as the chatter of small children than as momentous statements that could make a grown man helpless. It was not appropriate for a worthwhile and bighearted man like this stepfather to let himself be provoked by these insignificant teasings.

One more word on the name-calling and swearing: If either of these is a problem for you, there's another step we would recommend before you move on to the next chapter.

Make sure you are not triggering this behaviour by doing the same first.

Think carefully back to exactly what you said to your child just before you got the last few instances of these items. Was it something derogatory or critical, or even a name, like, 'Stupid!', 'Nitwit' or 'Fatso'? Did you swear first? Or did you give orders? Ask a question? Make a complaint? Did what you said have the word 'you' in it? These are all triggers, and by becoming aware of them you could gain some control over the distressing things your teenager is saying. You can probably turn on his or her problem talk by using these triggers, and decrease it by doing something different.

Ask yourself this question: 'If I *wanted* to get my son or daughter to swear or call me names, how would I do it?' Your answer to this may describe how you *are* doing it.

Having a sullen or belligerent attitude.

Sophie (16) has a sullen attitude. She always looks gloomy and ill at ease.

Timothy (14) has a belligerent attitude. He makes a gesture that makes me think he's going to hit me whenever I tell him something.

Tommy (15) sort of cringes and sneaks through the living room as if he thinks I'm going to hit him. I never have, and it makes me feel like a big monster.

If you're like us, you'll perceive a message behind these attitudes. It will seem to you that through these attitudes your adolescent is saying to you:

You're no good.

I'm unhappy and it's your fault.

You'd better watch out and treat me with kid gloves or you'll get hurt.

Please don't hit me, you bully!

Understanding these messages so well may be the way you invite your teenager to keep up attitudes like these. We suggest you become much more dense. If you think there may be a real problem behind this attitude, offer to help out if you can – once. After that we suggest you refuse to understand these subtle messages, and trust that if your child has real trouble and wants to bring it up with you, he or she will say something straight out.

Think over the attitude problem in the following way:

First, make sure you're not triggering this unpleasant attitude by being bossy, or saying derogatory things, or looking disapproving, angry or disappointed. In short, make sure *your* attitude is one of friendly courtesy.

If the attitude makes you feel afraid, as a belligerent attitude sometimes does, decide what you'll do if the worst comes to the worst and you actually do get hit, for instance – and then relax in the knowledge that you know just how you will act and so need not make any decisions about it. Once you've made this decision, fail to notice the belligerent gestures. In other words, if you're actually getting hit, do something effective for yourself, such as calling the police. If you're not, firmly drop the problem. Refuse to take the third alternative, of living in fear and worry about something you can't control.

Finally, check to see what you've been doing when you noticed the attitude – that pang of worry, guilt, anger, or fear you experience. That's your part in reinforcing the attitude you don't like. Decide to turn on any other response instead of one of these feelings. If it fits your life style, you might gear yourself up to run after the boy or girl to tickle him or her every time you notice the cringing, or the gloom or the abused look.

Sometimes parents reinforce unpleasant attitudes like these by taking them personally – by seeing the attitude as aimed directly at themselves. Thus if a son or daughter takes on a sad or sullen look, or says 'Good morning' in a low voice, the parent thinks this has something to do with him or her, and feels accused somehow. Now, this may be a completely accurate perception; your teenager may actually be feeling something negative towards you. It may also be a faulty perception; he or she may not be thinking of you at all, but simply have a sore toe or be half asleep. Whichever the case, for you to perceive the attitude as directed towards you is a mistake, because doing so gets you something you don't want; it hardens the attitude, encourages it to keep happening. Try instead letting it be all right whatever attitude your teenager has, so long as it does not directly injure you. You might decide that it's all right for each person in a family to have a different attitude. There could be a cheerful, a sullen, a grave and determined and a cranky one in your family – and as long as no one's being hurt, the variety in attitude could enrich the whole family.

After all, we see that different nations of the world tend to encourage different life styles. The people of one nation tend to be frank and open; other peoples are known as more gloomy, or reserved, or volatile or polite. Every one of these is a valid life attitude for a human being. You could accept that your son or daughter has what seems to you a gloomy, a sullen or a hostile attitude.

Steven (13) was a quiet, restrained boy who spoke very little. His stepmother was an open, highly expressive person herself, and it always seemed to her that Steven's silent, rather dour expression meant that things were going wrong for him and that it was her fault somehow. She had done many kindly things to win him over, but his silence, his gloomy looks, and especially the way he said 'Good morning' to her (like a robot, she felt) made her think he was antagonistic to her. She may have been right; what she did not see was that her anxious focus on Steven's attitude was locking that attitude in place, and that Steven may simply have had a different personal style from hers.

Abusing favours a parent has granted.

Let's consider one more set of problems that parents sometimes encourage by almost asking for them to happen. The following items seem to us like instances in which a teenager is abusing favours that a parent has implicitly or explicitly granted.

Borrows my car and doesn't take good care of it.

Borrows money and doesn't return it.

Uses my make-up and leaves it in a mess.

Leaves my tools out to be ruined.

Doesn't show up at the appointed place and time when I go to pick her up.

Doesn't return his library books and leaves me to pay the fine.

Orders me to take him here and there; doesn't ask courteously.

These items are alike in that almost any outsider would see that in a sense the parent is asking for the misbehaviour, while the parent is aware only of feeling frustrated, ill-treated, helpless, angry. We've been in this position ourselves and still feel amazed at how blind we were to the fact that we were *permitting* the misbehaviour.

One of our sons drove our car carelessly. He backed it into a post, denting the rear bumper, and declined to fix it. We were excited, upset, angry. He drove it carelessly again and ran it into a pile of bricks, smashing the front grill. We were upset and scolded him. Yet a third time, he drove it hard and fast without oil until it broke down, a total wreck. Throughout all of this it never occurred to us that we were giving him permission to use our car and that we didn't have to.

... *and reverse charges, please* ...

Do you do this sort of thing? If your daughter doesn't return money she has borrowed from you, have you continued to lend more before it's paid back? If your lad leaves your tools out, do you permit him to use them again before you feel good about it? If your daughter misuses your car, or your library card, or your typewriter, or any personal belongings of yours, do you continue to let her use them after the first time? If so, your permitting these things may be one of the triggers in bringing about the misbehaviour. By granting a favour after it's been abused and when nothing has been done to make it right, you invite continued abuse.

All of these are items that happen again and again, and their basic pattern is this:

1. Your teenager presses for some favour – either asks for it or simply takes it for granted (to use your car, to be picked up, to use your library card).

2. You grant it, either by giving direct permission or by simply not saying no.

3. Your son or daughter abuses the favour, but also expects it again.

4. You feel abused, mistreated, frustrated, angry – and yet you grant the same favour again.

   This pattern is based on some ideas in both your heads. They are ideas like these:

A parent belongs to his or her offspring.

138

A parent has no rights and must not be so selfish as to claim anything for him or herself.

A good parent is one who is ready to give him or herself over to any children they've chosen to have.

Having these ideas, the parent does give him or herself over, begins to feel natural resentment at being taken for granted, and then is liable to feel wrong and guilty for even feeling resentful.

Your continuing to agree to the favour *triggers* the misbehaviour, and your failing to take care of your self when it's been abused *reinforces* it.

The basic skill we recommend you learn in order to deal with being taken advantage of is that of *Refusing Favours*. Here's how to go about it.

First, think for a moment of all the different ways in which your particular son or daughter presses you for something. How does he or she say it?

Hey Mum, we're out of bread.

Dad, wake me up at seven, will you?

Dad, you can pick me up at the cinema at 11.30.

Can I borrow £5?

Mum, take me to the bike shop.

Dad, I'm taking the car tonight.

May I have a dog?

I'm bringing home a dog.

Am I going to have to drive that old banger of yours when I get my driving licence?

I want a new car when I pass my exams.

These are all situations in which, if you say yes, you're doing a favour. These are not things you owe to him or her; they're favours. And because they're favours, you can appropriately feel free to say yes or no to them.

As you think of these examples, notice whether you feel you *have* to say yes, or if your first impulse is to jump to take care of the request, without first considering whether you really want to or not. If you're doing this, you probably feel that it's your job to wait on your teenager, and your teenager may well feel it's his or her right to be waited on.

Notice that many of these are requests you might want to say yes to if the relationship were going well, and that you might resent if you were feeling unfairly treated in general. For example, 'Hey Mum, we're out of bread' sounds good coming from a cheerful boy who's just finished his share of the dishes; it grates coming in a demanding tone from someone who's done nothing but munch crisps in front of the TV all day while you've been doing your work. In the latter case, you may well feel like saying no. And certainly if the request has a negative history behind it, if it's in an area in which your son has repeatedly abused your permissiveness, something in you will want to refuse, and probably will keep wanting to refuse until things are put right.

> If Dave hasn't turned up when you've gone to pick him up in the past, you won't want to go to pick him up next time.

> If Sheila borrowed money from you before and didn't return it, something in you will want not to lend her any next time.

> If Gary has wrecked your car, or if you discover he's been trying to see whether it will do 100, or if he never refills the petrol tank, you may well want to say no the next time he asks for it.

> If Linda didn't take care of her fish, you may not want to get her a dog when she asks.

Our point is that every time you receive a request or a demand, something in you will know very well whether it *wants* to agree or not. In the past you may always have said yes because you thought somehow that you had to. From now on, whenever your son or daugher asks for something, *focus your attention on your inner signal-giver; find out whether it wants to say yes or no, and then follow its wishes.* This means that sometimes, probably when your youngster is pleasant to be with and you're feeling good about him or her, you will want to say yes, and you will do so. And at other times, you will refuse. Here's how to do the refusing.

First, if you're going to change what you do about favours, it's fair to let that person know that things will be different. Therefore tell him or her once, in an I-statement, what you plan to do. It can be short and sweet, and you can do it in a relaxed and kindly way.

Debbie, I'm dissatisfied with the fact that I sometimes say yes to favours when I really don't want to. I'm going to take care of myself and do favours for you only when I feel good about it, when I really want to.

Now, relax and go about your life – until the next request comes up. As soon as it does, STOP! Resist the urge to say yes without even thinking about it, and instead, ask yourself whether you *want* to grant it. If the answer is no, say in a gentle and relaxed tone:

No.

Then add the most honest and short I-statement reason you can think of for your not wanting to say yes.

Janet: You can pick me up at the Wimpy Bar.
Dad: No, Janet. I feel uncomfortable about the way I was asked.
Joe (at a restaurant): Mum, can I have your dessert?
Mother: No, Joe. I want it myself.
Jeff: I'm taking the car tonight.
Father: No, Jeff. I feel uneasy about your driving my car.
Barry: (whose father had agreed to pay him £3 for washing the car): Can I have my £3 in advance?
Father: No. I feel nervous wondering whether I'm going to get my side of the bargain.
Paul: Take me to the bike shop now.
Mother: No. I don't want to.
Marian: Mum, I need to take your camera to school for a project.
Mother: No. I don't like to lend my camera.

You may be tempted to pad your 'No' with extra explanations.

No, Joe, I'm hungry, and I especially like this kind of dessert, and you've already had yours, and it's not polite to ask for someone else's dessert, and besides, it has coconut in it and you don't like that.

Don't do it. Stick to your short, direct I-statement. The extra verbiage only muffles it. Don't give any other reasons, either. Reasons are appropriate for times when you're on good terms with your youngster and would really like to say yes but have some compelling reason not to, so you explain why you're saying no instead. We're talking here about times when something in you feels it's being walked on, and does not want to say yes. In this case, giving extra reasons only tells everyone that you do not feel you have a right to say no. Especially avoid the temptation to give reasons that aren't based on your own wants for yourself. For example, 'No, Joe, you know dessert will give you pimples.' Simply give your own personal reason, concisely, and then stop.

Your teenager may respond in any way from a cheery 'OK Mum' to a screaming tantrum; you may get no pressure at all to change your mind or you may get a great deal.

Once you've given your no, it's important to stand firm unless you honestly change your mind about wanting to grant the favour. If there's pressure to give in, listen quietly to what your son or daughter says or does, and then repeat your refusal courteously:

No, I don't want to.

No, I don't lend my camera.

No, I want it myself.

We've now mentioned five kinds of problem behaviour that parents often invite. At this point, please look over the remaining items on your parent's-life list to see if you might have been triggering or reinforcing them in the past.

Have you been triggering the behaviour before it starts by:

Using 'you's'?

Asking questions?

Giving orders?

Complaining?

Making derogatory remarks?

Doing basically the same kind of thing you complain of in your teenager, yourself, first?

Setting the situation up in some way that makes the behaviour more likely?

Have you been reinforcing the behaviour after it happens by giving negative attention:

Scolding? Punishing? Lecturing? Weeping?

Experiencing unpleasant emotions – anger, fear, worry, frustration?

Becoming upset? Glum? Anxious?

Use this chapter to work out how you will act, from now on:

Use I-statements when you're talking about anything that bothers you.

Set up the things in your life in such a way as to make them convenient and comfortable for you, without encouraging others to steal from you, take advantage of you and so on.

Decide upon how you will behave when troublesome items occur – in ways that do not include giving negative attention.

If parent's-life items continue to be a problem after you've sincerely stopped any triggering or reinforcing of them, go on to the assertive techniques of the next chapters. You'll be in a sound position to use them because you'll know you're not encouraging misbehaviour at the same time as you press your teenager to do better.

The only way we can see in which you might still be asking for these parent's-life items is by the old, well-known response we call *putting up with it*, and we'll be working on ways to change this next.

Chapter Nine

Standing up for yourself

If you've sincerely worked through the first eight chapters of this book, then at this point:

> You value your teenager's decision-making ability and are encouraging him or her to make the decisions that affect his or her own life. You are no longer trying to control your teenager's life, if you ever were.

> As much as possible, you are being a friend, wanting to see your teenager be happy in his or her own way. You see your teenager as competent and as able to run his or her own life, and you're interested to see how he or she does it.

> You have stopped any triggering or reinforcing of your teenager's troublesome behaviour.

> You are pleasant and courteous to your teenager, and you are continuing to provide a home and all the support that goes with it.

If you are doing these things, it seems to us that you are certainly respecting your son's or daugher's 'rights'. You are being fair and considerate and are not asking for mistreatment in any obvious way. If you're still having problems, then, it would seem that you are being treated unfairly, that *your* rights are not being respected. It's time to stand up for them.

Doing that can be one of the most rewarding enterprises in this book. It can bring about a much improved relationship with your son or daughter, a better feeling about yourself, some tense moments and some wonderful, exhilarating ones – and it can be fun. We hope you enjoy it all.

This part of the work is most effective with clear parent's-life items – things which, if a room mate of yours did them, would lead almost anyone to agree that you were being treated unfairly. It applies to items like these:

Runs up long distance phone bills without either asking your permission or paying you.

Makes a mess and doesn't clean it up.
Leaves his wet towels all over the bathroom.
Leaves the kitchen in a mess.
Leaves her dirty dishes all over the living room.
Doesn't clean up his dog's mess.

Doesn't take care of her dog.

Continues to steal your things.

Plays loud music on the stereo at all hours.

Stays out past a reasonable time and then breaks windows, locks, etc., getting in.

Sponges – lives with you and will neither go to school, work, nor contribute in any other way.

Won't do household jobs.

Brings friends into your house while you're not there.

Has parties in the house while you're at work, perhaps during school hours, perhaps involving drink, drugs, sex.

Grows marijuana in the house, or stores it in his room, putting you in an illegal position.

Persists in smoking in bed, even after burning holes in bed-clothes and furniture.

Knocks holes through plaster and doors, dents refrigerators, breaks tables and other furniture, when angry.

Your pregnant daughter moves her boyfriend in to live without asking your permission (or your son moves his pregnant girlfriend in).

Aspects of kid's-life items that you held in reserve because they do affect you directly are appropriate here too.

Please plan to spend some weeks, perhaps a month or two, making the shift into standing up on these items. We're aiming towards quite a basic change in your attitude – from feeling obliged and duty-bound about your teenager to feeling comfortable about taking care of yourself. That won't be achieved by going at it in a hurry, by suddenly throwing out a few assertive statements and then settling back into old ways. It is, rather, a slow, thoughtful, and persistent working at the steps, one after the other, that will do the job.

Look over you parent's-life list and pick an item at about middle range for you. We're going to take you through a series of escalating steps to use in dealing with this item. In the process of doing this you will learn a philosophy and technique for dealing with all of the parent's-life items on your list. The particular item you work on may resolve itself at any point along these steps, but it need not matter to you which step does it because you know you're going to stick at it until the problem is resolved for you.

The five major steps will be:

1. Establishing the fairness of what you want. This step will include an honest attempt to negotiate with your son or daughter; whether or not this succeeds, at the end of this step you will have made a clear statement of what you want.

The problem may be solved at this point. If not, move on to Step Two.

2. Standing up for what you want against your teenager's pressure to give in.

146

3. Repeating Step Two several times if the problem recurs. It is most likely that the problem will resolve itself here. However, if it does not, you go to Step Four.

4. Establishing credibility in your word, to prove you will do what you say you will do to get your rightful due.

5. A parental strike.

We will use as our main example in going through the steps the teenager's failure to contribute to the work load in the family. However, the approach we describe for this item applies for all of the parent's-life items. As you get experience with applying these principles to the first of the items on your parent's-life list, extend exactly the same procedure to the remaining items. Most parent's-life problems reduce to quite manageable proportions or disappear altogether when you conscientiously go through the first four of these steps. For those problems that don't it is appropriate to consider, as a last resort, the fifth and final step, the parental strike. We will talk about this in Chapter 10.

Suppose, then, that you're feeling unfairly treated because your teenager does not, will not, 'forgets' to, do anything to help out around the house.

Step One

First, to establish a sound basis for your campaign on this item, establish the fairness of what you want. This step may take some new communication skills on your part, so make sure you read the whole step over before you begin working on it.

This step is important because, although it may seem obvious to you that you are being unfairly treated, it is quite possible that your teenager believes he or she has a *right* to treat you in this way, or even that this is the way you *want* it. Now, it has been found that in any sort of encounter, the side that everyone knows is in the right has a tremendous advantage. You may have noticed, with animals, that even a small dog can chase a big one out of its garden – because both dogs know the small one is 'right'.

> Studies show that when two equally strong stickleback fish have a conflict, the fish who is guarding its own nest and therefore is in the 'right' *always* wins.

Your aim in this step, then, is simply to establish in your own and your teenager's mind the fairness and thus the rightness of what you want. Since the parent's-life items are all things in which

147

almost everyone in our society would agree you're being treated unfairly, you can expect that something in your youngster, too, will recognize the fairness of your want, if you present it in a non-accusing way. From then on, if your kid repeats the misbehaviour, he or she has to feel, not like a glamorous rebel against authority, but like someone who is doing an injustice. That doesn't feel nearly so good.

Don't count on your son or daughter's behaviour changing much as a result of this step. However, when you're finished with this step, you will have stated clearly what you think is fair, and your teenager will either have agreed or disagreed with your view of fairness or will have refused to talk about it with you. It makes little difference which happens, because the kid is likely to misbehave again in any case, but you will have established your concept of fairness, and that gives you a sound basis for taking the next steps.

Here's an effective way to carry out this step.

Pick a time when you are both reasonably relaxed, and in a courteous, friendly voice make a three-sentence announcement that *you are dissatisfied with the situation*, that *you want to see it changed*, and that *you would like help with it*. All three sentences should begin with 'I' and only the third sentence should have any 'you' or 'your' in it. They could go something like this:

Sentence 1. John, I'm feeling dissatisfied with:

the way the work load has been distributed here.

(or, depending upon the item you have picked to work on:)

so much noise from the stereo.

what's happening about the dog's mess.

the way my clothes have been disappearing.

finding people have been in the house while I'm out.

hearing so many four-letter words around here.

Sentence 2. I want a change in the situation so that it's more fair.

(or)

I definitely want a more fair arrangement in this matter.

Sentence 3. I'd like your ideas on how I could solve it.

(or)

I'd like some help from you in working out a change.

I'd appreciate any help you could give me on this.

I'd be interested if you have any suggestions that could help.

Your son's or daughter's response will either suggest to you some readiness to talk about it, to begin making a deal, or it will make you feel put off. If it sounds to you like a readiness to talk, begin working on a deal. It might go as it did for Gary's mother:

Mother: Gary, I'm dissatisifed with the way our house is always so messy and my feeling that I'm the only one who works on it. I want a more fair arrangement. I'd like some help from you in working out a change.
Gary: I don't like the house being so messy either. (Occasionally kids do say things like this.)
Mother: I'd like some help in setting up a better arrangement. (Stick to your subject: getting a more fair deal.)
Gary: Well, I won't be so messy from now on.
Mother: (consulting her own signal-giver) I want something more definite than that. I'd be willing to make dinners and clean the kitchen if you'd clean the living room and bathroom every week.
Gary: If I have to, I'd rather do the kitchen than the bathroom.
Mother: I'd feel good about that. That's a super arrangement.

If your son or daughter responds to your first three sentences in this way, congratulate yourself. You've just got a verbal agreement on what would be fair. You're perhaps more likely, though, to get a response that makes you feel put off. When you give your three sentences your teenager may try to shift the subject of the conversation from your wish for a more fair arrangement to something else, such as who gets the place dirty in the first place, or the fact that the vacuum is broken, or anything else to sidetrack you. Or he or she may simply walk out on you, or call you a name, or just grunt, or hang his or her head and look embarrassed. If any of this happens, simply keep pressing towards a deal by repeating variations of Sentence 3.

> I'd really like your help on this.

> I want some ideas on how I might solve this problem.

If, after three or four repetitions you still get nothing that sounds like cooperation, continue to repeat variations of Sentence 3 and begin adding preliminary negotiating offers, still as I-sentences.

> I'd be willing to make dinner every night if you'd take over the outdoor jobs.

> I'd feel good about it if you'd take care of keeping the living room clean.

> I'd feel all right if I could count on three hours of solid work from you every Saturday.

Or, if you're working on a different item:

> I'd enjoy having a dog if I knew you'd clean up the mess.

> I'd be willing to have the stereo on for two hours in the evening if I could count on quiet the rest of the time.

Make your statement, wait to see what the response is, and if it's another put-off, simply repeat some variation of your statement again.

Take your time at this: talk in a slow and relaxed way. Every time you make a fair and courteous statement like this and wait, there is a pressure on your teenager to respond, so let that pressure work. You might wait a full fifteen seconds between statements.

If you keep at it in this way, quietly and politely, ignoring for the moment any attempts to distract you and simply sticking to your statements, you may eventually get some response showing willingness to make a deal with you. For example:

Dave: Well, what do you want *me* to do about it? (Never mind the tone of voice. Stick to getting a verbal agreement if possible.)
Parent: I'd feel good if you looked after the front lawn.
Dave: I won't do slave work like that! (Never mind how reasonable

or unreasonable your teenager's remarks are. Stay focussed on setting up a fair arrangement.)

Parent: I want to be able to count on a fair share being done by everyone in the family.

Dave: Why don't you get Sally to do her share? (Never mind diversionary remarks like this; stick to getting an agreement.)

Parent: I'd feel better if the dinners were cooked, or the ironing done.

Dave: Oh . . . (four letter word)! I'll take the ironing then. (Never mind swearing and a reluctant tone at this time. Stick to getting the verbal agreement.)

Parent: I'd feel good about that.

If after fifteen or twenty minutes your son or daughter still won't even talk about what would be fair, or if he or she simply leaves the room or refuses outright to talk with you, then drop the subject for the moment, and be ready to repeat the whole step again in a few hours or the next day. *Make three such attempts* – more, if you want to – before you decide that your kid is not going to help you solve this problem. When you reach this point and feel you've given him or her ample chance to come up with something, then state clearly, once, what you think would be fair, and hence what you will expect, and then stop. Stay with I-statements and put in as few 'you's' as possible when you say this.

> I think it would be fair if I counted on you to take care of the living room every week, and that's what I'm going to do.

> I think it would be fair if I shopped for the groceries and paid for them and could count on you to bring them in and put them away. That's what I'll expect to happen.

> I think it would be fair if I knew that either you were getting yourself educated, or were paying for your room and board, or were taking charge of the work around the house. I'll expect one of those to happen.

> I think it would be fair if anything that gets broken around here is paid for, and I'll expect that.

If you've managed to get some sort of verbal agreement, finish up this step in a similar way by making one, clear, summary statement of what you will expect.

> I'll make the dinners, then, and I'll count on having the living room and the kitchen cleaned.

> I'll do my part, then, and I'll count on having the ironing done every week.

> I'll count on having no one but you in the house while I'm out, then.

> I'll expect anything that gets broken to be paid for, then.

> I'll be expecting freedom from the stereo, then, except between 9 and 11 p.m.

If you've really carried this step through sincerely, you will know at this time that you have established for everyone that you are fair, direct, and want a solution to this problem. You've also served a fair warning of what you expect. There's a bare possibility that simply doing this much will resolve the problem for you. Whether it does or not, though, you've still advanced your cause, because you have chosen the ground on which the encounter will occur, and it's one in which it's clear that *you're in the right.*

From now on, if you stand really firm, your son or daughter may very well want to agree with you, and if you can make it possible for him or her to do so without losing face or pride, the situation may go well.

In any case, after you've made your summary announcement, read over Step Two so that you'll be fully prepared for the next move. Prepare the short sentence we ask you to make in that step and store it in your memory. Then forget about the problem until you get the next 'twinge' about this item. Pay no attention to whether the teenager does the job or not. If he or she does do the job, pay no attention to the methods he or she uses. Do not check to see whether the job has been done, and do not remind your son or daughter. Rather, keep your attention on enjoying your own life, and as long as you are feeling comfortable, do nothing about the item.

At sometime, a few hours or a few days after you've stated what you want, your enjoyment and comfort is likely to be interrupted by the old, familiar 'twinge' about this item.

> If your son or daughter's job was to help with the work for a couple of hours on Saturday mornings, you will realize that he or she is already out of the house for the day with the work undone, and you'll feel a 'twinge' of pain or anxiety.

> If the job was to care for the garden, you'll glance out the window, notice the leaves are only half raked and the garden tools have been left lying out, and you'll feel a twinge.

If you've said you will expect no friends in the house while you're out, you'll see evidence that they have been in the house, and you'll feel a twinge.

If you've said you'd count on freedom from the stereo except in the evening, you'll hear a loud blast in the middle of the day, and you'll feel a twinge.

If you've said you'll expect your teenager's dog to be fed, you'll notice the dog is still hungry past its feeding time, and you'll feel a twinge.

(If you notice that the job is not done and you do not feel a twinge, but instead for some reason feel OK about it – do nothing! Your task is not to see that your kid does the job – rather, your task is to take care of your discomfort. If you don't get a twinge when you see the job isn't done, then presumably you're comfortable about things, and there's no problem. In short, we ask you to let the twinge, not the item itself, be your guide in proceeding.)

As soon as you feel a definite twinge because the item you're working on has happened again, move on to Step Two – *standing firm for what you want against pressure from your kid to back down.*

Step Two

The primary purposes of Step Two are to get practice in persisting and in avoiding being sidetracked. Accomplishing these two things will make your Step Two effort a success whether or not you get what you rightfully want at this point.

Here is what to do for Step Two.

Prepare ahead of time a short, clear I-statement describing what you will want to happen to ease your twinge if the want you described in Step One is not met. *Make sure there is no 'you' in the statement.*

If the item is failure to do a job, then say:

I'd like the kitchen cleaned up.

I want some solid help this morning.

I'm wanting the dog-mess cleaned up.

If the item is something that really can't be changed because it's already happened, then say:

I'd like to know no one is coming in the house without my permission.

I want to know I won't hear any four-letter words around here.

If your child has 'borrowed' something of yours without asking, then say:
I'd like my blouse back just as it was (washed and ironed) and I want to know no one is going to my wardrobe without asking me.
Or:
I want any dog in my house to be taken care of.

I'd like the money for this phone bill.

I want my house free of pot.

I'd like the hole in the wall repaired.

When you have designed your statement, memorize it and have it ready to use.

Now realize that in this matter you are standing up for a fair and essentially equal-rights arrangement between the two of you, and your kid needs to have you persevere in claiming this arrangement. However, he or she also needs to know you can and will be firm in taking care of yourself in this way, and it's part of the game to give you some resistance to test that firmness. Your teenager may throw you all sorts of hooks designed to pull you off the track and turn the conversation to something other than your want. Your job will be to keep your part of the conversation firmly on your want and resist all the tempting side issues your son or daughter will bring up.

You will start this conversation on the subject of *your* want; be determined that no other subject, no matter how important it may be at other times, will pull you away from your want until it has been satisfied.

Be prepared to concentrate your entire body to the task when you state your want. Don't call from the next room, or make your statement over your shoulder. Go into the room, get fairly close (three to five feet) and let your whole body face your child as you talk.

The very next time you see your son or daughter after you experience the twinge, go to him or her and make a *polite request.*

This is probably the only question we'll ever recommend you ask your teenager, and it has a purpose – not to get cooperation (it probably won't do that) but to lay a good base for the dialogue which will follow. It reminds your teenager that you feel you have a right, that you are courteous, and that you will continue to take care of yourself.

Barbara, will you please clean up the kitchen?

Jim, will you please take care of the garden?

Megan, will you please put my mind at ease about whether you'll be going to school or paying room and board?

Peter, will you please feed the dog?

Steve, will you please pay me for this phone bill?

Your son or daughter will make a response to your polite request that either makes you feel good, or leaves you still dissatisfied. If the response eases your twinge and makes you feel comfortable about the item, then simply give an I-message describing that comfortable feeling.

Dan: Of course, Dad, I forgot all about it. I'll do it right now.
Father: I'd like that.

Barbara: Oh, sorry about that, Mum. I was busy with something else, but the dishes will be done within half an hour.
Mother: I feel good about that.

Megan: Oh, I forgot to tell you, Dad. I saw my headmaster this morning and I'm starting back at school on Monday morning.
Father: I'm glad to hear about that.

It's more likely that your son or daughter's response will leave you still feeling much of your twinge, put off and doubtful about whether the job is going to be done and your want met. He or she may say something like:

But I have to do my homework now.

OK, OK, I'll do it later!

It's not my turn.

Why do I have to do all the dirty work?

or

I won't.

To .... with you! (or worse)

I'd pay you for the phone bill but I haven't got any money.

None of the subjects I can do at school are any good.

These are all hooks designed to pull you away from the subject of your want and into something else – into taking responsibility for your son's or daughter's homework, into dropping the conversation, into arguing about turns, or about whether this is dirty work and why it need be done at all, into scoldings and counter-defiance and explanations, and so on. You've already given your kid a very fair chance to bring up problems like this, in Step One, and if they come up now, it's fair to ignore them. Refuse to be pulled into any of these other subjects, and instead: Begin responding by using the *three-part assertive sentence*.

The *first* part of the sentence is meant to let your son or daughter know you heard him or her. It can have 'you's' in it, because it is to be simply a reflection of what you heard your child saying or expressing. To make this part of your sentence, simply listen to what your teenager says or does, summarize it for yourself, and then give it back. You'll find that phrases such as, 'I understand that...', 'You're saying that...', and sometimes simply, 'Mm hm', are good for beginning this part of the sentence.

I hear that you do have homework ...

I realize you want to do it later ...

You're saying it's not your turn ...

You wonder why you have to do it ...

You're saying you won't do it ...

    or

I understand that you don't have any money ...

You don't like your subjects ...

The *second* part of the sentence is the word 'and'. You may find yourself wanting to use 'but' instead. We find 'and' to be more effective. In this sentence we're asking you to express two wants or feelings, your child's and yours, and the word 'but' connecting them implies that the two are in conflict and only one or the other is really valid. The word 'and', on the other hand, implies that there are two wants and they can coexist. It bypasses any attempt to change this conversation into a conflict.

The *third* part of the sentence is the I-statement you have already prepared.

The total sentence, then, goes something like this:

(1)	(2)	(3)
I understand you want to do it later,	and	I want the kitchen cleaned up.
You're saying it's not your turn,	and	I want some solid help this morning.
You wonder why you have to do it,	and	I want the dog-mess cleaned up.

Your son or daughter will probably respond with another hook; you handle it in the same way, simply reflecting it back to him or her, adding an 'and', and then restating your basic I-statement. You can *keep your voice courteous and yourself comfortable* as you continue to respond in this way, because you don't have to put any energy into working out what to say (you already have your three-part pattern and your basic I-sentence) and you know that no matter how this particular incident turns out, you will continue to look after your want until it is satisfied. So you can't lose, and you are in a good position to remain calm and relaxed. You can let your youngster do all the shouting, acting out, worrying, manipulating and so on. This in itself is a tremendous change from the usual situation.

Be prepared for the many different kinds of hooks he or she may throw you. Here are some common ones we've heard, along with possible ways you might respond to them.

Teenager: You're always on at me!
You: You're saying I'm always on at you about something – and – I'd like the kitchen cleaned up.
Teenager: You don't care about me!
You: I see you think that I don't care about you – and – I'd like the kitchen cleaned up.
Teenager: Why do I have to do more than Carol?
You: Mm hm, you're wondering why Carol doesn't have to do more of the work – and – I'd like the kitchen cleaned up.
Teenager: You like her better than me!
You: I see you're thinking I like her better – and – I'd like the kitchen cleaned up.
Teenager: I'm not going to do that slave work!
You: Mm hm, I understand you won't do slave work – and – I'd like

the kitchen cleaned up.

Teenager: You're just saying what the social worker told you to.

You: Mm hm, you're hearing that I'm talking the way the social worker showed me – and – I want the kitchen cleaned up.

Notice that at this time:

> You need not answer questions.

> You need not justify your want.

> You need not prove you are fair or that you care.

The job is simply to be loyal to your inner being by sticking to your want.

If your child walks out on you – stomps off to his or her room, or runs out of the house – do not run after him or her, but simply go about your business until the next time the two of you meet. Then begin this new conversation by saying quietly: 'Nigel, I'd like the kitchen cleaned up.'

How long should you keep this up? Until you get a response *that eases your twinge* – that is, that leaves you feeling reasonably assured your want will be cared for – or, until you've gone through your three-part sentence twenty times. Count on your fingers as you give the sentences; this may keep you feeling calm and just preoccupied enough that you do not get pulled into any well-designed hooks thrown out to you.

If you go through this twenty times and your teenager is still refusing to take care of your want, stop the three-part sentence. At this point pay no attention to your teenager. Be especially sure you DO NOT GIVE ANY NEGATIVE ATTENTION WHAT-SOEVER. If you have feelings of discouragement or frustration now, turn them off, and allow yourself a feeling of satisfaction that you managed to give your three-part sentence all twenty times. Now either do the job yourself or take steps to get it done in some other way. You can do this cheerfully, because if you've completed this step, it is a success – no matter how your son or daughter responded and regardless of whether or not the job got done. Congratulate yourself, because you have stood up for your rights. Allow yourself to enjoy any feelings of confidence, even exhilaration, you may have experienced as you stood up in this way.

Step Three

Step Three is, essentially, to repeat Step Two the next time this same problem recurs.

Whether your original Step Two resulted in your teenager doing the job or not, you're likely to get the same old 'twinge' of discomfort at least one more time. Again,

> You will walk through the kitchen, notice it is a mess, and feel a twinge.
>
> You will realize that someone has been in your house while you were away and feel a twinge.
>
> You will get a bill for a long distance phone call you didn't make and you will feel a twinge.

As soon as you feel this twinge, remember that your job is to take care of it, and as your first step in doing so, turn to your youngster and again make your polite request:

'Barbara, will you please clean up the kitchen?'

You can count on the fact that your boy or girl was not comfortable when you went through Step Two the first time. We find that people in general, adults as well as young people, feel very uncomfortable saying 'No' to a fair, friendly, persistent statement like the one you made in Step Two. Even if your teenager put on a cocky face and resisted your appeal through the whole twenty sentences, you can be certain that he or she did not enjoy it. When this second time comes up, it will dawn on your son or daughter at about the second or third repetition of your sentence that that whole scene is about to repeat itself. Your teenager is likely to think, 'Oh, no, here we go again!' and may well opt to give you what you want gracefully rather than go through those uneasy and perhaps guilty feelings again – *if* you let him or her keep face doing it. That's one reason we ask you to stay courteous and relaxed, so the teenager will know he or she won't get crowed over after agreeing to do what you want. Instead, you let him or her know how good it makes you feel to have your want taken care of:

Teenager: I know, I know, I know; you want the kitchen cleaned! (going to do it)
You: I really feel good about your doing that.

You: . . . and I do want the money for this phone bill.
Teenager: Yeah, Dad, I heard you! I forgot to tell you about the call, but here's the money.
You: I'm glad and so relieved you've taken care of it.

Repeat Step Two several times, depending upon (a) whether

your teenager shows any signs of being ready to take care of you, and (b) whether you've really followed Step Two instructions thoroughly and been courteous, friendly, persistent, throughout. If you can see ways in which you slipped up, repeat this step again and again. Do it until you're utterly comfortable going through it.

'He's doing the dishes! Mum's fainted!'

It's very likely that by the time you've gone through these three steps the situation will have improved noticeably. Most of the families we are able to help show the bulk of their improvement within a few weeks or even days after the parents honestly (1) stop trying to control the kid's-life items, as in Chapters 2 to 4, and (2) make a firm stand, as we've described, for their rights on the parent's-life items.

If doing everything we've suggested so far has made this kind of difference for you, your main job from now on will be to maintain the progress you have made. You can do that by following these two rules for yourself:

> I will trust my youngster to make his or her own decisions on kid's-life items.

> Whenever I get a twinge about a parent's-life item, I will do something to take care of it. My first step in that direction can be to tell my child what I want, using the three-part assertive sentence.

We suggest that you read through the two steps still ahead in the following chapter. You may not actually have to use them, but knowing that you can and will if this is what it takes to take care of yourself can give you a worthwhile confidence. If you know with surety that you will stand up for yourself, it's far less likely that you will have to.

If your problem is still there after you've conscientiously gone through Steps 1, 2 and 3, we can think of two possible reasons. Both may be valid in your case. One is that you have not thoroughly enough followed through on the work of previous chapters, so that there is still too much intermixing of responsibility between you and your son and daughter. You may still be struggling in some way to control the kid's-life items, and perhaps you are still seeing your teenager as not able to make responsible decisions, or judging him or her, or feeling trapped yourself. If you have not taken care of these things, your son or daughter may not feel like taking care of you on these parent's-life items.

If you think something like this might be happening, review the earlier chapters of this book and give yourself time to get used to the philosophy they're based on. You may find the whole approach will work better for you a few months from now.

A second reason why these first three steps may not have changed the problem is that even now, *your son or daughter may not believe you really will stand up for yourself.* Maybe you weren't firm and clear when you went through the steps, or maybe he or she is preoccupied with something else entirely and didn't get the point for that reason. Maybe your teenager is getting so much safety out of being defined as the bad, irresponsible one that he or she can't or can't afford to see you as another, equal person with rights and needs of your own. In any case, it seems to us the teenager is in danger of growing up with the idea that other people don't matter and that he or she has a right to be taken care of without giving anything in return. That viewpoint won't serve any young person very well when he or she gets out in the world and you may be doing him or her a real favour by going ahead with the next steps and giving your teenager a chance to learn how to be an equal person.

Let's go ahead with the next steps, then, on the assumption that you have put a reasonable and sincere effort into the previous work in this book and that, for whatever reason, *your teenager still has not caught on to the fact that you are a real person with feelings and wants of your own, and that you will take care of yourself.*

Chapter Ten

Following through on your stand

You've now made a first, solid attempt to take care of yourself as far as these parent's-life items go. You did it by communicating to your son or daughter as clearly as you could what you want. This attempt failed to solve the problem for you, and you are now left with the responsibility of finding some other way of taking care of yourself.

We'll take a slightly different direction in this chapter. We'll be asking you to take some physical actions and, later, to use those physical actions in taking care of youself in relation to your child. We emphasize again, as in earlier chapters, that taking care of yourself in this relationship will take care of your child as well, in very important ways.

Before you begin Step Four, clear your mind for a shift to this new direction by doing a 'Minnesota Fats'.

Minnesota Fats was an ageing billiard champion who had been engaged in a contest with an able, younger opponent for many hours. They'd been playing all night and at last, near morning, it appeared that neither of the exhausted, bleary eyed, grimy men would be able to win. It was apparently a deadlock. At this point, Minnesota Fats left the game to go to the toilet for a few moments. Calmly he washed his face and hands, wet and combed his hair, and put on a fresh shirt he had ready for the occasion. Then he returned to the game and, physically and mentally refreshed, won it within a few shots.

At this point, you're in somewhat the same situation Minnesota Fats was. You've been coping with this problem with your son or daughter for a long time. You've just made a courageous stand which you hoped would solve that problem for you and it didn't. The whole situation may seem deadlocked to you. Therefore, it's time for a Minnesota Fats break. Take it by giving yourself some time entirely away from the situation; spend it doing something you really enjoy, and keep at it until you've had at least a few hours during which you were so engrossed in having a good time that you didn't even think about your teenager. Take a long, beautiful walk, or spend a day on the moors, or visit friends for a few days or a few hours – whatever you like to do to clear your mind. Then, refreshed by this interlude, set your mind on the next steps we will be suggesting in working on the whole problem.

If, at this point in your work your teenager still persists in doing things on your parent's-life list, he or she seems to be still wanting to exert power over you. And, evidently, he or she is able to do this through knowing what pushes your button and what you will do when it is pushed. You are predictable. Ironically, it is likely that one way in which you are predictable is that if your son or daughter persists long enough and with enough unpleasantness, you will ultimately go along with his or her plans just to get some peace. Step Four will be to establish an entirely new notion in your youngster's mind, namely, that whatever you say, you will stick with regardless of his or her level of effort to get you to change. In other words, his or her old prediction about how you will act will fail.

We think it is very important to let your teenager become acquainted with a new, somewhat unpredictable, you. Thus we urge you, before beginning the next step in this chapter, to *prepare yourself to have some fun becoming a generally more daring, unpredictable, spontaneous and zany person than you have been.*

Up to now, the following statements have probably been true of what happens between you and your teenager.

> *Your adolescent* does the unmanageable, unpredictable, crazy things and *you* have the role of worried, responsible one.

> When you and your adolescent talk together, you both talk about and focus on what *he or she* is doing, what he or she wants, how he or she feels – and what *you* do, want, and feel, has little or no part in the conversation.

> *You* worry about what your adolescent is going to do, and *he or she* does not worry about what *you* will do at all, because he or she sees you as a stable, entirely predictable person who has things all worked out.

163

Let's reverse this at least in part, and get the two of you on a more equal basis.

Here is how we suggest that you do that.

Imagine that for many years you've been a prisoner in a chain gang. You've had the same duties in this gang for so long that you no longer even see the situation, the duties, the other prisoners, the fairness or unfairness of the way things are done, but simply operate automatically, doggedly doing the tasks you think you have to do. Now imagine that suddenly you are set free. You're still in the same physical situation, but you're now free – to stay in this situation or to go, to do the same old tasks or to change to something new, to reassess your whole situation as a free person. As this free person, look around in your life now and begin speaking to yourself, over and over, in these sentences:

I'm free to do as I wish; what do I want to do right now – for the next five minutes?
Run?
Talk?
Lie down and rest?
Make up a little dance?
See how many colours I can see without changing position?
Nothing?

I'm free to do as I wish; what do I want to do for the next few weeks or months?
Buy a typewriter?
Play the stock market?

Lose twenty pounds?
Take up wood carving?

I'm free to do as I wish; what would I do if I were a bit zany?
Run about on all fours?
Change jobs?
Stay up all night listening to records?
Laugh?

As a very small child you undoubtedly had plenty of ideas about things you wanted to do. The ability to think as you did then is not lost; it's there to be used whenever you decide to tap into it again.

I'm free to do as I wish; what would I do right now if I were five years old?
Stretch up and see if I can touch the ceiling?
Run under the sprinkler and cool off?
Dive into deep snow in my bathing suit? (One of us did just that.)
Run away from my children for a few days? (Yes, one of us did that too.)

Give yourself lots of leeway when you answer these questions – let the answers be as crazy as you can make them. Then pick some of the craziest and do them. It could be something like these examples we've invented:

You are Tony's mother and he comes home after 3 a.m. one night. He comes in as quietly as possible so he won't be caught and scolded with, 'You were supposed to be home by twelve', 'You're late', 'Where have you been?', 'You're staying in'. As he opens the front door he is amazed to hear wild Mexican music, and then to see you lying on the floor writing busily, surrounded by a litter of papers, empty coffee cups, and records. He blurts out, 'What are you doing?' (almost the first time he has ever asked you what you were doing). 'I've decided to stay up until I learn all the Spanish words to my records', you say.

You are driving your daughter to school, as you usually do on your way to work. At a crossroads where you usually turn left, you turn right. Your daughter asks incredulously, 'Where are you going, Dad?' (almost the first time she has ever asked you where you were going). You say, 'I'm taking the River Road "shortcut". I've guessed the mileage and I want to see how close I come.'

Your daughter Alison has tried the bathroom door several times in the last half hour and notices that you are still in there. Finally she says, 'Mum, what are you doing in there?' (almost the first time she has ever asked you why you're taking so long in the bathroom). You say, 'I'm taking a bubble bath and eating a spicy pizza I made.'

These are all 'a little bit crazy' things; we're asking you to do lots of them and, in fact, make a habit of doing them all the time. How many you do is limited only by your ability to think of them, and we have found that once you let yourself think of a few, they can start coming more and more easily. It's so much fun to do them, once you've begun, that it's easy to get into a habit of doing them, not just for your teenager, but because they are fun, for you.

Your going 'crazy' in this way acts to correct the balance in what's happening between you and your teenager, so that:

At least part of the time, *you* do the unmanageable, unpredictable, zany things, leaving the role of worried, responsible one to your teenager, if he or she wants it.

At least part of the time, when you talk together, you both focus on what *you* want, how *you* are doing, how *you* feel.

At least part of the time, *you* do no worrying at all. If there's any worrying going on, *your kid* does it – wondering what you will do next, because he or she begins to see you as an unpredictable person. As a human being, you always were unpredictable, but your teenager didn't know it, and to find this out about you is one of the nicest things for him or her to learn. Your boy or girl does not have you all worked out. As you will notice as you do this step, *neither do you*, and that's nice to find out about yourself, too.

You've already made a start at doing all this, in Chapter 6. There we asked you to get into a habit of consulting yourself on how you are feeling and what you'd like to do, or be, or have. We asked you to do some small, spontaneous, fun things and to express your inner signal giver by dropping in spontaneous I-sentences every once in a while during the day: 'I feel', 'I like', 'I want', and 'I'm going to'.

Now it's time to weigh-up all of this. If you work at it seriously, you will find yourself feeling more and more free with it, more and more comfortable talking in this way in front of your teenager, and in front of his or her friends and, for that matter, in front of the neighbours, the people at the shopping centre and all of your relatives.

Notice that we're not asking you to do anything to hurt other people. We're simply asking that you yourself do things that will make *you* feel happier, freer, more confident that you can count on yourself to take care of your own wants.

When you've practised being more spontaneous and unpredictable enough to feel quite comfortable about it add Step Four.

Step Four

In this step your job is to *establish the credibility of your word*, to prove to your kid that you will do what you say you will. In this step we're preparing for a confrontation and ultimatum, a parental strike, to be used if serious problems aren't resolved before things go that far. Well before that real ultimatum, it is vital that your teenager believes that you will definitely do whatever you say you will. Only if your teenager believes that, can he or she believe you when you make a serious statement of your intention to 'strike'. If, when you give this ultimatum, the young person thinks that you do not mean it and that you may give in, he or she can play brinkmanship with you, and continue misbehaviour just to see whether you mean it. On the other hand, if the young person knows very well it is truly an ultimatum, because *you always do what you say you will*, then he or she can make a responsible choice, either to go along with it, or to refuse it and take the consequences.

This step, then, is a pre-ultimatum move designed to establish in your son or daughter's mind that you can be counted on to do what you say you will.

For this step, we ask you to do a series of dramatic demonstrations. It will take courage and ingenuity on your part; it may be fun as well. Here's how to do it.

First, pick some minor situation that bothers you. It need not be anything your teenager does, although it might be. Let it be a small thing that happens fairly often, such as:

> Somebody always leaves the toothpaste out on the sink instead of putting it away in the drawer.

> The children get into noisy arguments when we're all at the supper table.

> Things keep getting left on the stairs, where I'm afraid I'll trip on them going up and down.

Second, use all your imagination to think of something you could do if this were to happen again that would meet the following conditions:

a. It would make you feel better to do it; it would ease your twinge.

b. It would hurt no one, nor would it be aimed directly at your youngster.

c. It could be a little zany – unreasonable, outrageous, unexpected or startling.

d. It would be dramatic enough that others, especially your son or daughter, would be sure to notice it.

e. It would have some relationship to the incident which bothers you, without blaming anyone else for it or giving anyone negative attention.

f. It is something you have full power to accomplish yourself.

Some things you might decide to do, for example, for the incidents we've mentioned:

> Write a large notice on the bathroom mirror – in toothpaste – that you want the toothpaste put away.

> Pick up your dinner, ceremoniously arrange it on a tray, carry it into your bedroom and shut the door, and eat it alone and in peace and quiet.

> Take anything you find on the stairway and throw it into the garden, or on the roof, or into the bath. (This would not be directed at your teenager's clothes but at any clothes on the stairway.)

We'll talk more about the kinds of things you can do after it's clear what to do with them.

When you've thought of something like this that you would be willing to do, hold it in mind, and then:

Third, announce to your family what you want as far as this item goes – in a mild, relaxed I-statement, with no you's.

> I'd like the toothpaste kept in the drawer.

> I really want peace and a friendly atmosphere at the supper table.

> I want the stairway clear of things.

This is a kind of mini-establishing what you think is fair.

Fourth, wait until the situation comes up again (you can be reasonably sure that it will).

Fifth, repeat to your family what you want in this situation, and this time *tell them what you will do if you don't get what you want.*

> I really want the toothpaste kept in the drawer. If that doesn't happen, I'll write on the mirror in toothpaste.

> I really want peace and quiet at the table. If I don't get it, I'll take my dinner into the bedroom and eat by myself.

I want the stairway clear. If I find it cluttered, I'll throw the things into the bath.

At this point, you may be saying to yourself, 'It isn't logical to spread toothpaste on the mirror if I want the bathroom clean and neat.' True, it isn't logical, from the rather narrow perspective of the cleanliness of the bathroom. But your goal is much broader than the cleanliness of your bathroom, and from that broad perspective, other, narrower views of logic could well be quite illogical. Don't be trapped by logic, consistency and so on. The toothpaste is a vehicle towards establishing your credibility.

Sixth, wait until the situation arises again (and after your last statement it is almost sure to come), and when it does – do what you said you would do. Do it with enjoyment.

And *seventh*, consider this step a success if you begin to experience a sense of exhilaration and even power as you do these things. We're aiming towards a feeling of *freedom* (you are not trapped by your teenager or the situation), of *competence* (you can do things to take care of yourself), and of *exhilaration* (it's appropriate to feel joyous and expansive about all that you are free and able to do).

Now, what kinds of things can you pick to do?

Choose something that you can do *in order to make yourself feel better*. Do not do it in order to teach your child a lesson, nor to get even, nor to push him or her into doing anything. Pick something you can do for yourself and then forget.

Make sure that what you decide to do is directed at things rather than at people, and that when the time comes to do it, you act firmly and surely, without hesitation. In this step we're asking you to take physical action, and physical action can have either of two very different effects on the other people in your life, depending on how it's done. If you take action in an angry or upset, impulsive way, or if you direct it at another person or his or her belongings, it can excite others to retaliate and take action or even become violent against *you*. On the other hand, if you perform your action with a sure, firm, deliberate feeling, so that it's clearly something you're doing on purpose and feel you have a right to do, and if it does not invade another's person or property, it can inspire others, too, to behave more responsibly. That's one reason why we ask you never to attack your child physically, and if you do decide to take action involving his or her possessions, to make a clear statement ahead of time that you mean to do so, and be sure it seems fair to you. If you do things this way you're unlikely to precipitate violence.

Make sure that each thing you decide to do is a specific and one-time action, and not a long term, repeated activity. We've seen parents get into drawn out contests by saying something like, 'If you won't do the garden, I won't do the washing.' The young responds with, 'If you won't do the washing, I won't do the garden', and the situation becomes a contest. Neither washing nor garden gets done for a long time and your resentment builds. Make your thing something you do once and that's the end of the incident. That way, if the annoying problem comes up again, you're free to handle it in some new way, and meanwhile you're eased of your twinge and can go about your life.

> If the garden isn't done by four, I'll feel embarrassed to have anyone to see me, and I'll wear a mask when the visitors come over tonight.

Make each thing as zany and dramatic as you can be comfortable with. We can't tell you just how far to go in this direction because what's zany and dramatic depends so much on what the atmosphere has been in your family and what your particular style has been. In a family that is generally soft-spoken, polite and reserved, some very small, only mildly dramatic things may have a large impact. In a different family, say one in which four or five children have taken over and are openly running a single parent, it may take much more dramatic behaviour to attract attention. For example:

Mrs I. had always been very quiet and deferential. It was a dramatic event for her family when, in front of them all, she announced that she would take an extra pat of butter for her baked potato and did so.

Mrs B. told her family she was going to run away for three days. Then she packed and did it.

171

In general, we think that the kind of parent who would read this book can't lose by being as zany and dramatic as possible. It's likely that a problem in the past has been that you've leaned too far in the dutiful, conventional direction and let your adolescent do all the unpredictable behaving. Consider, then, doing some things you've never done before and enjoying the feeling of daring that it can give you.

And finally, don't worry too much about getting the things you choose exactly right. It's better to do some and have them backfire a little than to hold off and continue to feel walked on.

Here are some things that desperate parents we have helped have come up with or that we have suggested for them. Some of these break the rules we've just set up, and no doubt that reduced their effectiveness somewhat, and yet – doing them at all can be a great improvement over what has been going on.

Quiet Mr D. felt nearly overwhelmed because his very boisterous stepchildren openly ignored or insulted and were contemptuous of him. When we suggested he do something dramatic to demonstrate to them that he was there and would do whatever he said he would, he recalled that he had bought them the TV set they were using, and that it was kept in an upstairs room. In fact, the noise from this TV and the fact that the children listened to it and ignored him was one of his complaints. He decided that the next time the children ignored or insulted him, he could easily pick up the TV, take it to the window, and throw it out into the garden.

'I want to feel that I'm treated like a person around here. If I get the feeling I'm not, I'll throw the TV out the window.'

A sensitive and vital woman, Mrs W. told her family she was heartily dissatisfied with being awakened nearly every night by someone's entering the house around two or three in the morning, and that the next time she was woken up like that she would scream. A few days later her son, Matthew (16), once again came in very late. She got out of bed, put on a dressing gown, walked out into the middle of the street, and screamed three times at the top of her voice, 'Matthew W. is not fair!' Then she returned to the house and went to bed.

Mrs T. had told everyone in the family how she felt about the rubbish bin — that she wanted it emptied, and that she felt it was unfair for her to do it when she had so many other tasks for the family. We suggested that the next time she noticed the unemptied rubbish bin, she say, 'If the rubbish isn't emptied by this afternoon, I'll serve it up for dinner.' Then she was to get out the best silver and dishes, and very artistically serve the family bowls of sloppy coffee grounds, orange and potato peels, and so on.

Mrs G. decided, in a session one of us had with her and Mr G., to say, 'I get so upset when the washing is just thrown on the floor instead of being put in the hamper, that I think the next time I find it I'll throw it out of the window into the front garden.' Her husband's clothes were included in the total that had been appearing on the floor. He responded, 'Fair enough.'

Mr M. wanted to get more exercise into his daily life and decided to use this approach to a problem he had been having. He told his kids, 'I have trouble driving the car when there's fighting and shouting going on. If it happens again, I will get out and walk.'

'If these cleaning things are left in the hall once again, I'll throw the whole cupboard-full away.'

When you've done several things like this, you may sense that your teenager is beginning to see you in a slightly different way. You may catch a puzzled or thoughtful expression when your son or daughter looks at you, or he or she may begin to consult you, asking you whether you'll be home or whether you'll be making dinner, or do an occasional considerate thing for you, like asking whether you'd like some of the snack he's making for himself. Even more important, you will find that you are becoming more confident and comfortable doing active things to take care of yourself. You'll begin to notice that when a problematic situation comes up and you feel a twinge, your first thought is, 'What can I do to make this better for me?' rather than, 'My kid is misbehaving.' Hope may come to you, too, a surge of joyous feeling that says, 'I do not have to put up with unfair treatment! I can always take care of myself!'

Now begin gradually to extend this same approach to other, somewhat more important things that have bothered you, ultimately including the parent's-life items that are still a problem for you.

Here are a few examples of how parents can use the Step Four approach to work on these parent's-life items if previous steps do not resolve them:

Andy, I really want freedom from the dog's mess left lying around so long. I will not tolerate them any longer. If I see any more of them, I will find another home for the dog.

173

Sandy, I feel bad about having people in my house when I don't know about it. If I get any feeling at all that it's happening again, I'll arrange to have a housekeeper in for a week.

Paul, if I don't get the money for the long distance calls to Scotland by Tuesday, I will have to put a lock on the phone.

Carol, I want to feel secure about my things. If I miss any more of my money or clothes, I will definitely call the police and ask them to investigate.

'If there's any more serious damage to the house, I'll sell it!'

The four steps you have just completed comprise our basic recommendations for dealing with the parent's-life items on your list. If you've worked through this whole book thus far, and then actually followed through on several items using the Step Four approach, we think you will find that you are no longer feeling nearly so helpless about problems as you once did, that instead you are feeling more and more able to take care of yourself when they come up. By this time you'll be coming through to your son or daughter not only as someone who deeply respects your teenager's rights, but as a more definite person yourself, someone more to be respected than before. For the great majority of readers of this book, the problems you've been having will have changed for the better. The task from now on is one of maintaining this improvement and continuing to practise the things you have learned.

For a few parents in unusually difficult situations, we will describe a further step to be taken – a parental strike. We advise that you go onto this step only if you have sincerely worked through everything else in the book, and then only if the problems you experience are serious and quite painful to you. This step can sometimes help when all else has failed, and we certainly think you

174

should take it rather than continuing in a situation that is demeaning or painful to you. However, we don't recommend using it if other approaches seem to be helping, or if you have only minor problems left. In that case, it would be better to practise more thoroughly the skills you have already covered, or, perhaps, leave things as they are for a time to see how they settle down.

Mrs T. was feeling unbearably pressured by the things her daughter, Natalie (16) was doing, and she asked for help in finding a foster home for her. We asked her to come for guidance instead, and she agreed. Natalie herself refused regular counselling, but her mother came and worked hard at the kinds of things we talk about in this book. After a few months almost all of the problems she had experienced were gone, and she was living on good terms with her daughter. She actually enjoyed warm talks with her and a feeling that she and Natalie cared about each other. Two things continued to bother her: Natalie clearly was going on with an active sexual life (which shocked and worried her mother), and she continued to strew her clothes all over the hallway (which merely annoyed her mother). Mrs T. decided not to push for further changes but to rest content with the progress both she and Natalie had made. She decided to take care of herself as far as Natalie's sex life went by helping Natalie to get birth control pills in order to assuage her (the mother's) anxiety about possible pregnancy. She also decided to imagine that she had a pet bear who naturally strewed things about, but was worth keeping anyway. She took care of herself by putting a large cardboard box in the cupboard at the end of the hall and scooping all the clothes into it when she came home at the end of her working day.

For this parent, it would not have been appropriate to go on to Step Five. She had few problems left, and it seemed likely she could handle those by working further on what we've already covered in this book. For some other parents, however, this step may be the only thing definite enough to make a difference. It seems appropriate for situations in which, for example, a young person is running the family like a dictator, or is doing adult things (like having sex, or even babies, or driving cars) without taking responsibility for them, or is sponging on the family and refusing to do anything to care for him or herself. Teenagers are just people, and like everyone else, they, too, can become dictators, tyrants, manipulators, if the situation allows for it. In such cases strong measures like a parental strike may be needed to get everyone back onto a saner level.

Carolyn (16) ignored her parents most of the time; when she did condescend to speak to them it was usually to express contempt or to give them orders. She was already feeling entirely free on kid's-life items, and she simply ignored her parents' attempts to stand up for themselves on parent's-life items. She seemed so deeply convinced that they had no rights that a strike may have been the only way they could show her otherwise.

175

Gary (15) had got his fifteen-year old girl friend pregnant and then informed his family that he was moving her in to live with them. His parents objected, saying, among other things, that they did not like the idea of the two under-age youngsters having sex in their son's bedroom. Gary responded to all their objections with tantrums and dire threats to kill himself if he did not get his way. He did concede, though, that he and his girlfriend would not occupy the same bedroom; she, he said, would take over his mother's sewing room. He proceeded to move her and many bags and boxes in the next day. An hour or so later the two youngsters went to Gary's mother to ask her what dinner was going to be.

These parents had so little successful experience in standing up for themselves, and the situation was developing so fast, that we felt a build-up of assertive techniques would not be enough. We recommended an immediate and firm parental strike, in which it would be made clear to Gary that he could choose to live as an adult with his girlfriend only if he took responsibility for it, and that living as a child-couple in his parents' home was not one of his choices.

Barbara (15) refused to go to school and instead invited rather tough friends in to live it up with her while her mother was at work. Her mother told her what she wanted, made agreements with her, went to negotiate with the school and other officials to get Barbara what she said she wanted. Barbara always cooperated in working out agreements, and promised to abide by them, but then went on in her disturbing ways exactly as before. We agreed with the housemistress that it was appropriate for Barbara's mother to strike.

We ask you to think your situation over and decide what direction is right for you to take now. If things have improved through your work in this book, you are doing something very right, and the job is to learn to do it even more thoroughly. On the other hand, if parent's-life items are still a major problem for you, and a strike seems fair, then go ahead with Step Five feeling definite and confident about it.

Step Five

Up to now, everything we've suggested for you to do presupposes that you are going to continue your part in a conventional parent-child relationship – that is, that you will live with your adolescent and provide him or her not only with material things – a home, food, clothes, perhaps an allowance and so on – but also with more intangible forms of parental support. However, if it's to be fair, the parent-child relationship, like any other, should be a two-way street. The parent should experience rewards for providing care and support, and the rewards – knowing the teenager is developing well, a reasonably good relationship, a feeling of loving and being loved – ought to be great enough that the parent enjoys the supporting. If you're not getting the rewards, then we think you're being disloyal to yourself: you're making yourself give without reasonable return. Your child, too, is probably not benefitting fully from the relationship. We think that a teenager who steadfastly refuses to join in a cooperative relationship with the parents has some important learning to do and may be best able to do it through living without some or all of the parental support you have been giving.

If this relationship were with any other person we can think of – a friend, a boss or employee, a neighbour, a spouse – and you were still feeling unfairly treated after so much hard work, you might well have considered pulling back from it somehow or completely withdrawing. We see no valid reason why this relationship should be treated any differently, especially since your child becoming independent some day is an inherent aim in this particular relationship from the beginning. In fact, looking at this as simply a relationship between two human beings *both of whom are free to leave it if they wish* may be the best thing for it. Therefore our basic recommendation for Step Five is that you *announce your intention of withdrawing from the conventional parent-child relationship in some way unless something happens to make you happier in it. Then carry this through.*

We realize that for some parents, this is not at all simple, even when children are far overstepping reasonable boundaries. You may be one of these parents; you may have compelling reasons for wanting to keep a traditional parent-child relationship going with your teenager in spite of all the trouble you're experiencing. One of those reasons may be the attitude of our society right now. Nowadays if a spouse treats you as your teenager has been doing, society – by which we mean your relatives, friends, and the legal establishment – will generally support you in getting a divorce. However, that same society may go to extra lengths to persuade you that you should and must continue to be responsible for your child and put up with the mistreatment no matter how bad it is. Unless you are rich enough to pay for private boarding schools, or poor enough to receive state aid, you're likely to have a much harder time withdrawing from this relationship than from any other we know of.

This attitude of society can be a real pressure upon you; it can make you afraid to behave as your common sense tells you is right. Both you and your child are aware of this attitude, and we think that's one of the factors that helps *create* the parent-child relationship as a one-way street. In other words, *both you and your teenager may believe that you are not free to leave the relationship,* and because of this belief you may be putting up with more and your son or daughter may be dishing out more than would otherwise be the case.

Taking Step Five may make for an improved relationship between you and your teenager, or it may not. Be prepared to have it turn out either way, and to feel good about carrying it through in any case. In our opinion, it's better to feel free to take Step Five, no matter how it turns out, than to continue to feel trapped in a situation that's making you feel unhappy.

Begin this step with one or two partial strikes.

Think over the parental support things you do 'for' your kid – things into which you would not put so much energy if it were not for him or her. For you, these may be things like the following:

> Talking with him or her – feeling concerned, interested, affectionate.
> Making supper every night.
> Buying groceries for two (or four, or six).
> Teaching him or her to drive.
> Allowing him or her to have a key to the house.
> Giving him or her an allowance, lunch money, money for clothes.
> Doing the washing.
> Coming home every night whether you want to or not.
> Making a special room available in the house for this person.
> Providing a place to live in – a house or flat.

Now decide that from now on, you will do *only what you want to* of these things.

The next time you find yourself about to do one or another of these things, ask yourself whether you feel like doing it. If you do, go ahead and do it. If not, say:

> I'm going to skip making supper tonight. (Or – I'm not going to buy groceries this week.) It makes me feel I give and don't get anything back.

> I'll not be taking you to practise driving tomorrow. I feel I've been doing more than my share, and I'm not going to keep giving unless things become more fair in the home.

> I'm not going to do your washing this week. I feel put upon when I give and don't see any return. I'm not going to do that to myself.

Then go about your business. If your teenager does something – such as doing his or her task, or being pleasant to you, or whatever – that makes you feel like doing the thing after all, then say:

> I'm feeling good about doing this after all.

If your son or daughter does not do this, keep your word. Abstain from these things you have been doing 'for' him or her unless you really feel like doing them.

Sometimes parents hesitate to 'strike' in this way because they're taking care of *several* people, and they feel they can't stop doing things for one without depriving the others, too. Please do not decide you must put up with unfair treatment because of this. Use your head to work out a way of striking that you feel *would* be fair to the others, if you easily can. If you can't, then we recommend that you strike anyway. This may inconvenience the others in the family (it may also motivate them to take some responsibility for helping you resolve this problem!) – but we think that is better than being disloyal to your inner self by giving up on taking care of it.

Here are a few examples of how parents can make a partial strike by withholding something they have been providing.

Andy (15) and his parents seemed to be in a contest over when he was to come in at night. The parents wanted the house locked at midnight. Andy regularly missed this time by anywhere from five minutes to many hours, and his mother regularly spent sleepless nights because she couldn't relax until she knew everywhere was locked up. At last she decided to take care of herself by getting out of the contest. She couldn't quite bring herself to leave Andy to fend for himself, but she said, 'This house is definitely closed after midnight. If you're not in at that time, I'll put your sleeping bag out and expect not to be disturbed until morning.'

Every time Linda (14) ran away, her parents worried about her welfare and felt painfully uncertain about whether she would return. They tried to find their daughter and urged her, through her friends, to come home. However, her father began to feel resentful at going through this ordeal so often, and realized he felt it was unfair to him and Linda's mother. He told his daughter, 'Linda, it is a real hassle to me every time you run away. Next time it happens I want a complete break from you and from the hassle for three days. I want you to stay out of the house for at least that long.'

For several months Pete's parents had done everything they could think of to 'help' Pete (15), who had taken to missing school, coming in very late at night, bringing strangers into the house while his parents were at work, and so on. He snubbed and ignored his parents and would not contribute to family life in any way. His parents asked what was troubling him; they took him to a social worker and went to school consultations to help work out plans he might like. Nothing they did seemed to make any difference. At last the father became disgusted. He decided he wanted to continue supporting Peter as far as supplying a home and groceries, but that he would no longer invest himself — his interest and attention — without any return. Therefore he stopped talking to Pete — at all. The boy was very surprised at this, and made the first positive changes anyone had seen — in order to get back on speaking terms with his father.

179

Tony's mother was nearly wild with worry about his activities, which included violent behaviour at home (breaking furniture if he did not like what his parents said), using and probably dealing in drugs from the house, loud stereo at all hours, and nightly absences of many hours. At one point she began to wonder why she was putting so much of her life into the situation when Tony (16) showed no signs of wanting or appreciating her. She told him, 'Tony, I've provided a room for you for a long time, but at the same time I've always wanted a sewing room for myself. I want some signs that you want me to be your mother, and if I don't get them I'll stop supplying the room for you. I'll make it into a sewing room for myself.'

In these partial strikes you're making the clearest possible announcement that you want a change. If you are doing the things we have described so far in this book, you've been outstandingly fair, persistent, and respectful of your teenager's rights in leading up to it. If you do not get a favourable response to this plea, it's time for a more total strike, one which involves some separation.

The first move in this strike is the hardest: it is to *decide what kind of separation you can and would be willing to bring about.* It's hard because the idea of 'throwing my child out' can have the sound of abandoning a helpless waif to misfortune, and none of us is willing to do that. Nonetheless, seeing our kids as helpless waifs is one of the habits that has brought about so much trouble in the first place, so we recommend you change to a different picture of what you will be doing. Ask yourself seriously, 'How would I act if my child, behaving just as he or she is, were an equal age adult in my home?', 'How would I act if my youngster were nineteen?' Then act accordingly; treat your child as you would treat an adult.

There are several kinds of separation you could go for.

You could arrange for your teenager to live with a relative.

Mr and Mrs A's son (16) was running wild. The parents told him that spending the summer at his uncle's farm, working for his keep, was a possibility for him, and that unless they felt better about him within a week, that was the only possibility they were providing; living at home would not be one of his options.

Legally, a parent can provide for the support of a minor child in any suitable way of the parent's choosing. You do not have to provide that support under the same roof with you.

You could send your child to a boarding school.

If you can afford it and your child wants to do this, it could be a satisfactory solution for you. If your child doesn't want this, the situation may be different. Legally you are on firm ground since you have the authority to decide such things for your minor child.

180

However, boarding schools will often refuse to enrol unwilling students.

You could give your child permission to go and live with another family, in another household.

Eric (16) thought his friend's parents were 'simply marvellous' and his friend's older sister had grown up and left home, leaving a spare bedroom. Eric negotiated with his friend's mother to be able to live with them and pay £15 a week room and board from his after-school job. Eric's parents agreed. (Within four months Eric wanted to come home and his parents agreed. He was a different boy!)

Boys and girls frequently know of families who would be willing to have them stay with them, either with or without your financial contribution. You might even know of a family with a problem similar to yours that would be willing to swap children.

This kind of resolution, in which your son or daughter lives with another family not related to yours, has a very important advantage. It is immediately obvious to an adolescent that he or she must make that family actively want to continue having him or her live with them. Almost certainly your son or daughter knows how to make the family want to continue with the arrangement and the actual doing of it is excellent practice for adult living.

You could separate from your teenager but continue to give some financial support.

Alison (16) had a boyfriend and a circle of friends outside the family, and did little with her mother except fight. Her mother was unhappy in this situation, and Alison was hostile about having to be home at all. They talked it over, and Alison's mother decided to give Alison £100 a month until she reached eighteen, and to allow her to make her own arrangements about where to live.

You could declare to the local authorities that your child is out of your parental control, that you want him or her made a ward of the court, and that you will not continue living with him or her.

Local authorities (and police) may try to get you to change your mind and may even tell you that what you are proposing cannot be done. Generally, though, it can. Your child will probably be made the subject of a care order by the local authority and you may be asked to contribute financially. However, the closer your child is getting to eighteen, the less enthusiastic the authorities will be about doing anything like this.

You could pure-and-simply throw your child out.

If your son or daughter is legally an adult either because he or she has reached the age of eighteen or is emancipated (eg by being married) then this possibility is perfectly within your legal right. If your kid is a minor, then taking this action would not be legal and we would not recommend it, any more than we would recommend your going 80 miles an hour in your car. If you decide to take this kind of action bear in mind that it is not legal and that as a result there may be consequences for you. You may decide that the risk is worth it to you. We have noticed that many people who are under eighteen go on their own every year – some by their own choice, some because they've been 'thrown out' by their parents. We tend not to hear about them because they go one by one without publicity and so on, but there's a whole segment of society that lives in this way. Some of them return home after a time; others go on to make their way on their own. Many become successful business and family persons.

Perry (16) spent most of his time going around with a rather tough group inclined to petty lawbreaking. He would neither go to school, get a job, nor help around the house. He used the home only as a sort of convenient pad, coming in and out as he wished and incidentally littering the place with pornographic literature and objects like torn-apart wallets that had the look of being stolen property. His parents' attempts to get a better deal had no apparent effect. At last, when Perry phoned home after an absence of several days, his father told him to stay away.

After you've decided what you are willing to do, confront your son or daughter once again, this time with a statement that has two important parts.

In the first part tell him or her *what you want.*

In the second part say exactly *what you will do* if you do not get what you want *by a certain time.*

> *Alice, I want an equal relationship with you in which each of us makes a contribution. As I see it, your part is to get yourself educated or else contribute to room and board, and to help out here at home. If I don't feel you're doing your part by a week from now, I will no longer live with you.*

> *Ben, I'm still unhappy living with you. I want help with keeping the place reasonably neat, and a more pleasant atmosphere. If after two weeks I still don't feel I'm getting it, I will set it up so you can live with your uncle, if you like. In any case I will no longer provide for you here.*

> *Carol, I'm simply not happy living with you this way. If things aren't better within a few days, I'll say: I won't play ball any more; the deal's off. I'm willing to contribute something to your support wherever you're living, until you're eighteen, and I will want you out of the house.*

Once you've made this announcement, meaning it, wait until the end of the time you have set. If the situation improves enough to satisfy you by that time, fine. You've accomplished a change and the only job now is to continue to stand up for yourself. If the situation has not improved by that time, *do* whatever you said you would do. Do it without dramatics, guilt, hesitation or doubt.

Mrs. S. told her son (16) that unless she felt a major improvement in the situation, she wanted him out by the end of June. On the first day of July, having seen no change, she packed all of his things in cardboard cartons and put them outside, locked the house and went about her business. (Her son picked up his things, moved in with friends several years older, got a job as a mechanic and became self-supporting. No one knows why he never did this while at home, but an improvement in the situation was felt by all concerned.)

Kay (17) held open house in her bedroom for her boyfriend, by whom she was pregnant. He came in and out and spent the night as he pleased, even though Kay's mother, Mrs. L., said, 'If this happens one more time, I want you both moved out of my house.' He did come in again without permission, and when Mrs. L. said, 'I want you both out,' the boyfriend shoved her. Mrs. L. called the police. When they came, she agreed not to charge the boyfriend with assault for the shoving if the two young people would leave. The police supervised their move to a friend's flat.

Moving your son or daughter out of the house is probably *not* the end of the story. Your strike has more moves.

The first one is to *hold a positive state of mind in the period immediately after the separation*. Hopefully, when you took action to get your teenager out you were seeing him or her as a person able to care for him or herself, and you felt matter-of-fact and good about your right to be treated fairly. Maintain these attitudes against the pressures which may assail you now. A load of guilt can come down upon parents who have stood up for themselves as you have, especially if they are women, and children and society in general often play powerfully upon that guilt to persuade you to change your mind. Be prepared to stand firm and feel relaxed even against:

Phone calls from neighbours or perhaps from parents of the family your son or daughter is staying with, telling you how wonderful he or she is and how you too could be a good parent if you would only do so and so. (They won't use exactly these words but you will get the idea.)

Phone calls from friends of your teenager who ask to speak

with him or her as if they did not know the situation, and then begin pressurizing you to change your mind, telling you how wonderful, scared, loving, disturbed, etc., your son or daughter is.

Pressure from *your* parents or other relatives who say, 'You can't do this to your own child . . .' 'What will happen to him or her?'

(If this happens, you might tell these relatives that it would be all right with you if they would like your son or daughter to live with them.)

Phone calls from police.

(As in the case of calls from neighbours and other 'concerned' outsiders, the police at this point will probably have heard only your child's story. Since you will have gone through all of the earlier steps in this book by now, and will not have taken this Step Five action for anything trivial, your side of the story will very probably induce understanding and perhaps even help from the police.)

The other, and last, important part of your strike is to *be true to yourself when, as almost always happens, you and your child get in touch again.* A few days or a few weeks after separating, you're likely to be talking together again, either because your youngster phones you, or because you make the first move and contact him or her. When that happens, it's possible that you may learn that your son or daughter is well satisfied with being away and, in his or her own eyes, is doing fine. If this happens, keep in mind what you're after, and if it is a happy, relaxed long term relationship, be friendly and treat your son or daughter as you would any other dear, adult and independent friend. It's more likely that your child will turn out to be not so satisfied with being away, and will ask for financial help or ask you to take him or her back into the house. If this happens, remember to *consult your inner being* to decide how you feel about it. If that inner being feels good about it, consider giving the financial help requested. If that inner being feels comfortably sure things can really be better, then consider living together again. Tell him or her that you definitely want to be treated fairly, and that as long as you feel you are, he or she is welcome to return. If your inner being tells you nothing has changed and you'll be expected to do all the giving again, say, 'No.' It's not too different from a situation in which you and a spouse have separated for some reason. Once that separation has occurred, you have the right to stay apart or go back together as long as it *feels right to you.*

Chapter Eleven

A look ahead

You've now read through, and perhaps worked through, a whole book's worth of ideas for relating to your teenager in a different way. What can you reasonably look forward to after taking the trouble to learn and to follow this programme? How is your child likely to respond to all this?

In everything we've recommended we've assumed that you would like a positive relationship with your child in say ten years from now. That is very likely to happen if you've done what we have suggested in this book – even if you've gone all the way, through Chapter 10, Step Five.

Parents sometimes undertake the things we suggest with trepidation. They're afraid that if they drop their controls over kid's-life items their youngsters will run wild, or feel unloved, or become alienated from their parents. They're afraid that if they stand up for themselves on parent's-life items the youngsters will be angry, or feel deprived, or reject them. These are parents' fears. However, what actually happens when they go ahead with this programme is almost always the reverse of these fears. The adolescents become less wild and more responsible; they know they are cared for and they feel closer to their parents. Rather than feeling angry, deprived, or rejecting, they tend eventually to feel respectful towards their parents.

The immediate results of using this approach are often a brief resistance and then very quick improvement in the parent-child relationship. When you begin to stand up for yourself, for example, your teenager may sulk, or get excited, may make scenes, may even walk out on you. This lasts *until your teenager becomes convinced that you mean it and that he or she cannot make you give in.* At that point you may unexpectedly get smiles and a relaxed and happy demeanour as the teenager begins to cooperate in ways he or she knows are right. This cheerful, cooperative behaviour tends to last until something once again suggests that you are caving in and will put up with unfair treatment. It's almost as if the young person *wants* the limit you set and feels happy and satisfied at getting it. We've seen this happen time and again.

Tom (16), doing some carpentry work for his weekly household contribution, was making the place ring with four-letter words as he missed nails and had to pull them out. His father said, 'Tom, I want freedom from four-letter words.' Tom responded with a muttered curse. His father said, 'I realize you're angry — and I do want freedom from four-letter words.' At this, Tom slammed his hammer down and left the house, apparently in a fury. Fifteen minutes later he returned, took up his hammer, and was soon heard whistling happily as he worked, with no sign of resentment.

Andy's mother was much disturbed by Andy's late nights, but she dreaded doing anything about it. She had told Andy (15) many times that she wanted the house locked up by midnight; he had completely ignored these statements. She was afraid that if she went any further he would feel angry, or rejected, there would be a scene, she would feel like a bad mother, and so on. Finally, though, she geared herself up to say, 'Andy, this house is definitely locked at midnight. If you're not in by then, I'll put your sleeping bag out.' Then came the response she had been so dreading: Andy thought for a moment, and then he said, 'OK, Mum. That's fair.'

The longer term results of going ahead with this programme are an improved relationship between two independent people, the parent and the young person, and often more closeness than before.

After years of having a very hard time living with their son, Michael's parents finally, when he reached eighteen, threw him out. Michael left the house, but after three weeks he came back and asked if he could live at home while he was going to school. His parents said, 'The rules are still the same, and everyone who lives here has to follow them.' Michael agreed to this, moved back in, and from then on, as if by magic, was very pleasant to live with! He and his parents became closer than they had ever been. Apparently it took his eighteenth birthday to convince his parents that they had a right to stand up for themselves and mean it, and Michael responded well to finally getting this firmness from them.

Steven's parents bewailed the fact that Steven (17) never wanted to go anywhere or do anything with them. However, as part of the programme in this book, they stopped insisting that he do so, and began going on outings without him, simply inviting Steven to come if he wished but not pressing him at all. The fourth or fifth

187

such outing without Steven was a weekend spent camping. As the rest of the family sat around the campfire on Friday night, they were beautifully surprised to hear a car pull up and Steven and a friend get out and join them — because they wanted to come. *The relaxed, pleasant, accepting way they all felt towards each other that evening was much nearer what the parents wanted than the strained ways they had felt when they forced Steven to come with them.*

In some situations, particularly if parents have a hard time using this approach and must move into it very slowly, the results seem not so positive at first, and the relationship shows its improvement later. We think that even if you and your child part company and live apart for many months, acting according to the philosophy in this book is likely to get you a positive relationship later on. The parent-child relationship can be very intense – so intense that none of you may understand or be easy with it in the teen years. When the high charge of it dissipates a little and you can all get a better perspective on it, it's likely that you will make friends again. We've known many situations in which a man or woman of 20, 25 or older 'comes home again' in the sense of meeting the parents anew and making peace with them. If you want that sort of thing to happen, stay open to the possibility; it's likely to come.

If you've stayed with us all this way and sincerely worked through this book, we think it's time for you to give yourself thanks and appreciation for having done and understood so much. We believe you have probably made a major turn-around in your way of relating with your son or daughter. You may now have a strong, comfortable feeling that:

> Upset and crisis between you and your kid presents an opportunity for *you* to grow and change.
>
> You are an equal human being, with equal human rights.
>
> Your youngster is a competent and worthy person.
>
> You are competent too, and there is no situation in which you are helpless; there is always something *you* can do to help yourself.
>
> Your job is to fulfil, express, take care of your inner being.
>
> You are responsible for what *you* do.
>
> Your teenager is responsible for what he or she does.

Having come this far, your task now is to maintain these attitudes. Basically, they come down to two principles:

Seeing your son or daughter as a capable, worthy being.

Believing he or she is able, trustworthy, and responsible.

Communicating that belief to him or her by:
1. Saying directly, 'I trust you to make the right decision for yourself.'
2. Listening with respect – that is, while assuming that he or she can solve his or her own problems.
3. Enjoying your teenager's decision making.

Feeling comfortable about standing up for fair treatment for yourself.

To agree with these in principle is easy; to learn to live them in all the different situations life presents you with is difficult. It's for that reason we suggest that you reread this book every few months or so as long as there is tension in the situation between you and your child.

. . . .

We'd be interested to learn how this approach works for you – what success and what, if any, problems you have in using it. If you want to comment on your experience, or have questions about any part of this book, feel free to write to us. If you'll enclose a self-addressed, stamped envelope we will do our best to respond to you. Address us through our publisher, Exley Publications, 16 Chalk Hill, Watford, Herts WD1 4BN.

Our good wishes to you in your endeavour to bring about greater happiness for yourself and your teenager!

Bob and Jean Bayard

Questions parents ask

Isn't it my job to guide my child? Doesn't he need my guidance?

Indeed, yes, we think your son does need your guidance. However, no matter what you do, your son is likely to notice and be influenced by it; in that sense you can't help but guide him. What is important is where your guidance points – whether it says to your son, 'Follow my decisions because I know best and you can't make good decisions', or whether it says, 'You can make your own good decisions.'

To provide the best guidance, you must let go and trust your son to run his life. Don't let go of your ability to control things, though. Turn it back on yourself and use it to get into your own life everything you want.

Shouldn't my husband and I be consistent with each other?

We think consistency is very important, but not consistency of the sort that decrees you and your spouse must handle everything in the same way. The two of you are different people, with different wants and different feelings. Further, for both of you, those wants and feelings are constantly changing. So it usually doesn't work to require consistency in the sense that you both reach the same decisions about how to handle things.

There's another kind of consistency that's much more meaningful. Basically, it is being *consistent with yourself* in the sense of always being guided by your own feelings and wants, and knowing that no matter how the situation changes, you can count on yourself to take care of yourself. If you're consistent in this way, your wants and feelings may change, and your behaviour will be changeable to fit them, but you'll be consistently true to yourself. Your doing this is important for both you and your teenager.

Further, if you're loyal to yourself in this sense, and one of your deep wants is a happy relationship with your spouse, you'll be loyal to him in that you will want his ways of doing things to work well, and you will not sabotage them in any way. You'll trust your spouse to be able to handle problems that come up for him, in his own unique way.

Aren't parents supposed to set limits? How can I do that if I'm not even going to try to control what she does?

Yes, it does seem important to set limits. You can do so by setting limits, not on how your child will behave, but on *how you will be treated*. You can communicate clearly what kind of treatment you want, make a firm stand to get it, and, finally, let it be known what you will do to take care of yourself if you do not get it.

Isn't my daughter my responsibility? She didn't ask to be born.

We've heard both parents and children make this 'didn't ask to be born' or 'didn't ask to be adopted' remark, usually to justify a one-way relationship in which the parent feels guilty and obliged and the child feels resentful about not being given more. The remark sounds illogical to us; in the context in which it is used here, you didn't ask to be born either. We think of being born rather as a gift – and the essence of the gift is the right and obligation to be responsible for one's own self. What else does any human being have?

No, we think your child is not your responsibility, because she is not your possession. Your child is responsible for him or herself; you are responsible for yourself.

Isn't it selfish to take care of myself?

No. In the sense in which we describe it here, it's just the reverse.

Being unselfish and caring for others seems to us to be the highest form of human living. There's something almost paradoxical about it, though. It seems to be meaningful only if you give to others *because you want to* – that is, if doing so is at the same time a taking care of yourself, so that you're giving because it makes you feel good to see the other person happy. If you give out of duty, because you should, or while grudging the giving, or expecting some return, the giving becomes something different.

We think that it's important to learn this kind of giving because-you-want-to, and that a first step in this direction is learning to take care of yourself. It is our experience that when people become sensitive to and loyal to their own wants, they then find that one of the deepest of those wants is to help others, to love and live cooperatively with them. Then taking care of others turns out to be the deepest form of taking care of oneself.

This is a hard time in the world for young people to grow up in; I feel sorry for my daughter and want to help her.

We can certainly understand feeling sorry, but at the same time, it is a damaging point of view to take towards your daughter. She'd be better off if you let her know you believed she could get on in life just fine.

What about my daughter's self image? I often tell her I love her so she'll know she's cared for.

We agree that a young girl's self image and her feeling able to cope is very important. So the question is: What can you, the parent, do to improve that self esteem and your daughter's feeling of being able to cope? The best thing we see that will help is your changing your picture of your daughter so that you see her as someone who is capable, and holding to that view, letting all of your actions be guided by it.

How can my *changing help my son? Can I make any difference by myself if he won't try to change too?*

Yes, you can do much by yourself.

Some of your son's misbehaviour may be done in relation to whatever way you're behaving. If you change what you do, he will no longer be able to act in the same way, and from your point of view, his new behaviour is likely to be an improvement.

Some of his misbehaviour may stem straight and simply from the way he is, separate from you. You can learn to stop adding your useless worry to these ways of acting.

And certainly, you can learn to take responsibility for making your own life happy. That not only helps you, but it's probably the one most effective thing you can do to maximize the chances of your son's changing in a positive direction.

Do you mean just let them run wild and don't care about them?

It is one thing to say, in effect, 'Go ahead and do whatever you want. I don't care.' It is another to say, 'I am worried that if you do such and such, you will suffer in some way because of it, and I have faith in your ability to do what is best for you. And I do care for your well being.' It is, of course, the latter view that we are encouraging.

But what about being close? We used to be close, but he's pulled away.

When you were close, you were big, he was small. You said what was what and he generally did as you said. The teenage years are a preparation for a time when you will both be big and neither will say what is to be what for the other. Therefore he is pulling away from the 'me small' role and getting ready for the 'me big' time. This pulling away is natural and usually temporary. Be patient and the closeness is likely to return in a new, adult form.

What about the dangers? I'm afraid to let my son do what he wants because he might get hurt.

We care deeply about the dangers – enough to say a sometimes painful truth: Your continuing to try to control your son pushes him closer into danger. Your giving your teenager responsibility for his

own actions enables him to develop the best protection against danger: a clear-thinking intelligence that's geared to take care of itself.

What if my spouse won't cooperate with me in using this approach?

We have two important things to say here.
1. The principles we've described in this book apply not only to teenagers. They work in all sorts of other relationships as well. If the way your spouse relates to you and/or the kids is a problem for you, list those problems, divide them into spouse's-life and my-own-life items, and use all the principles in this book to work them out.
2. Make sure you 'let' your spouse and your child have their own relationship in whatever way seems best to them. For example, if you want to get along with your lad in a relaxed and affectionate way and are doing it, and your spouse and your son seem to relate to each other through orders, resentments, recriminations – let them. Stick to taking care of problems that impinge on your life and the way in which you relate to others.

Even if your spouse is cooperating but not doing it 'right' as you are, don't be the enforcer, but let your spouse do things the way it suits him or her.

Don't parents have any rights?

How could you ever doubt it?
Of course you have rights – and it's your job to champion them!

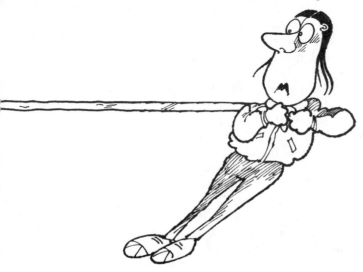

Some parents and how they coped

A Parent Who Coped Twice

Even parents who have a very hard time dropping controls over their children's lives can eventually become comfortable doing so and benefit from it. For Mrs. F., this took diligent and persistent work, but her eventual success was worth it.

She had been widowed when her two children were quite young, and was supporting the family and her invalid father on her widow's pension. Things had gone well until Gary, the younger child, was 14. Until then he had generally been obedient to his mother and was no problem either at school or at home. For example, although he preferred to go out to play after school, he grumblingly but obediently did his homework first. Then things changed. He began refusing to do his homework until after dinner, then occasionally not at all. Over a period of a few months his school performance went from satisfactory to poor, with some discipline problems and extensive truancy as well. In addition, he began to spend time with another boy with whom he started getting into mischief in the neighbourhood.

Mrs. F., a very gentle person, very early in Gary's 'problem' time found herself quite helpless to make any difference in his behaviour, despite scolding, pleadings, tears, appeals to honour the memory of his father and so on. Both Mrs. F. and Gary seemed to believe that if he did well in school and generally behaved himself he was doing it for her rather than for himself.

After a particularly trying session with Gary's teacher, to whom Gary had been impudent, Mrs. F. phoned asking for counselling help, and we began working with her and Gary. Soon, however, Gary began 'forgetting' to come to our meetings, and finally said he would not come at all. We did as we usually do when this happens – continued to work with Mrs. F. Like many of the parents we work with, Mrs. F. had much difficulty at first in giving up the idea that she should be able to control Gary's activities. Gradually, however, the reality of her powerlessness convinced her to begin trying something different, and she slowly and tentatively began applying the approach we describe in this book. Then one early July day, things seemed to take a turn for the worse. (They often do, as described in Chapter 4.) Gary and a friend were taken to the Police Station for throwing lighted fireworks into passing cars. He therefore had to suffer the full impact of the Juvenile Court system. As a consequence, he was ordered to go to an Attendance Centre for a number of weeks on Saturday afternoons.

During the rest of the summer and into autumn, Mrs. F. slowly but steadily moved to let Gary's decisions be his own. During this same time Gary slowly but just as steadily began to become more responsible. Although he was still acting up somewhat the problems steadily diminished until by the spring he was no longer failing in anything, was not getting into trouble in school or elsewhere, and he and his mother were on excellent, loving terms.

Happy ending of the story – right? Wrong.

At about this time Gary's older sister, who was then just turning 17, began to show some different behaviour. Up to this time she had been no trouble at all to her mother, had done well in school, treated her invalid grandfather well – in short, the kind of teenager any parent would find comfortable to be with. Then Sally made some startling changes, at least from her mother's point of view. She began missing school. In the past she had been interested in boys, but they were always the 'nice' boys, ones that her mother approved of, and she wasn't heavily involved with them. Now, she became very much interested in a boy several years older than her who lived down the street and who would come home roaring drunk in his old truck. She became involved with him sexually, in such a flagrant way that her mother was bound to find out. One day, when her mother was out but her grandfather was home in his bedroom right next to hers, she brought the boy into her bedroom for a noisy, graphically sexual session that she certainly knew her grandfather would report to Mrs. F.

At this point, Mrs. F. again came for counselling, on this new problem, and Sally also agreed to come in. The two of them had always been quite close and affectionate, and they reaffirmed their feelings of affection for each other, and Sally said that she would give up this boyfriend. However, very shortly thereafter, she stopped coming to the sessions and began seeing the same boy surreptitiously. Mrs. F. was distraught. Despite the fact that she had gone through the same kind of thing with Gary and had finally come to feel contented about dropping her controls over him, she was still caught in the helpless struggle to control Sally. It was almost as though she were starting afresh. But again, diligently and persistently, she worked at learning to drop her controlling habits. In the meantime, Sally did give up that boy friend but instead picked up another one who was 21 years old and was, in fact, put in an open prison shortly after Sally met him. Here he could receive phone calls at certain times, and Sally spent long periods talking with him on the phone, incurring substantial phone bills in the process.

We worked with Mrs. F. to turn over to Sally complete responsibility for her own life, including her love life. Mrs. F. concentrated on things like making sure she wasn't paying phone bills for her daughter's calls to the boy friend.

(In a bit of throw-back to her old, controlling ways, Mrs. F. was thinking of making Sally give up her job, ostensibly 'so she could study more', but really so that she wouldn't be able to pay for the phone bills and the mother could then use her inability to pay for the calls as an excuse to insist on Sally's not calling the boy friend. Fortunately it was rather easy to convince Mrs. F. that this devious ploy probably wouldn't work.)

For Mrs. F., the second time was just about as difficult as the first time. As with the first time, though, she did eventually succeed and by the time her daughter was 18 and had left school the two of them were on very good terms, somewhat as they had been when Sally was younger, but without the adult-child flavour of those times. Rather, it was more like two loving grown-ups relating to each other. At this point, Sally is continuing with her education at a local college, is living at home for the time being, no longer has 'raunchy' boy friends, and Mrs. F. is quite satisfied with the way things have worked out. Sally gave up the 'raunchy' boy friends quite spontaneously, and in fact one day casually remarked to her mother that, 'I don't think he (the incarcerated one) is the right kind of bloke for me.'

A Wholehearted Effort

Mr. and Mrs. B. had what could have been a very troubled

198

situation. We tell their story in some detail to illustrate what can happen when parents put themselves wholeheartedly into changing the way things are going.

Andy (12) had already been driving both his parents and his teachers to distraction for years before we saw him. His parents reported that he was out of their control. Whenever they tried to guide or correct him, he became violent and did things like smashing the car windscreen, hitting his parents' Alsatian dogs, threatening bodily harm to the rest of the family. These incidents often ended with Mr. B.'s hitting the boy and Mrs. B. scolding him for defying her. He had been expelled from two schools because he was as unmanageable at school as at home, and the headmaster at the third school advised the parents to put him in a mental hospital for a month's observation.

Andy's setting a poor example for his younger brother Dennis (9) and using Dennis' things without asking was one of the big issues for his parents. One day when Andy calmly picked up his brother's guitar, his father told him he couldn't have it. Andy responded with sarcasm and threats which infuriated his father and then, as the argument escalated, he seized his mother's very pregnant pet cat and raced towards the front garden with it, crying out that he would throw it over the fence into the street if his father didn't shut up. Mr. B. caught him just in time to save the cat and, as he did, gave Andy a hearty thump across the back. Andy immediately called the police to complain that he was being beaten. When the police came, he told them he was so angry that he was going to kill his parents that night.

In working with this situation, we gave due thought to the idea of a psychiatric unit because of Andy's threats and his history of wild behaviour. However, we felt we'd much rather help the family live together happily. Two factors influenced us to take this latter direction.

1. Despite all his wild talk, Andy had never actually harmed anyone. The dogs he hit (he slapped them with an open hand) were big and strong and did not look cowed. He had managed to run at precisely the right speed to get himself stopped before actually throwing the cat over the fence. He had not broken the car windscreen deliberately but rather by accident in the course of an unrelated scene.

2. We could see things the parents were doing which, if they changed, might make a definite difference in the way things went. Further, the parents were eager to work at making things better. They were miserable in their current situation, and at the same

199

time they certainly did not want to send their boy away. Mr. B. said, 'I'll do anything!' We took him at his word, and gave both parents definite instructions to try out.

First, we asked both of them to drop some of their behaviour, promising that we would coach them on things they could do instead. Mr. B. agreed not to hit Andy again, no matter how intense the provocation (Dad's hitting was giving Andy a model for violence and he was making full use of it). Mrs. B. agreed to abstain from scolding regardless of what Andy did.

Andy had refused to go to school the day we saw the family, and was playing about the house as we talked. We next told the parents, in Andy's presence, that they were breaking the law by allowing him to stay away from school, that they had no power to make him go, and that since they had already told him to go to school, they should from now on pay *absolutely no attention* to him during school hours. They were to act as though he were not there. (This was designed to deprive Andy of the attention he usually got when he stayed home from school.)

Each parent then made a separate list of the things Andy did that bothered him or her. Each came up with at least eighteen items. With their permission, we list some of them here.

Mr. B.'s list:

Yells at his mother, which infuriates me.

Always contrary. If we all want to go out for fish and chips, he has to have a hamburger.

Doesn't feel he has to do any work around the house.

Breaks things when he gets angry.

Embarrasses me by throwing fits and tantrums when we go out.

Phones his grandmother long distance and complains about us.

Steals things out of my room. Takes my tools without asking and I never see them again.

Expects me to jump to take him to places when and where he wants to go.

Mrs. B.'s list:

Won't get up in time for school. Forgets to bring his homework home so that he won't have to do it.

Leaves a big mess in the kitchen every morning.

Goes off without asking when he knows we're going somewhere.

Doesn't feed the dogs (his job), and is mean to them.

Leaves the bathroom in a mess (leaves his dirty clothes lying all around, and doesn't unplug the bath).

Walks in and changes the TV channel while I'm watching it.

Is a total idiot when I have company. I feel so ashamed of him.

Acts like an animal when we go out to eat. When we go out with him my stomach is in such a knot I don't enjoy it when we get there.

When I'm on the phone he yells on purpose so I can't hear.

Keeps wanting to go places and won't take no for an answer.

Both parents had these items on their lists, in different words:

Doesn't clean up his side of the boys' bedroom.

Spits everywhere.

Hits the dogs when he's mad.

Won't go to bed on time.

Eggs Dennis into doing dangerous things: stealing, playing with fire or knives, throwing stones, etc.

For the first week, we worked with Mr. and Mrs. B. on the kid's-life items on their lists. Here's what they did about some of them:

Mr. B.'s complaint that Andy yells at his mother.

Mr. B. agreed to stay out of whatever happened between his wife and Andy. He decided that when Andy's yelling at Mrs. B. bothered him, he would walk out of the room and get busy in his workshop.

Andy's not cleaning his share of the boys' bedroom.

Both parents told both of their sons that they felt the boys could be trusted to work out a way of caring for their room, and that they (the parents) were going to stay out of the problem.

Andy's refusing to get up in time for school or to bring home his homework.

Mrs. B. told Andy firmly that from now on she was out of the school situation, and would leave it to him and his teachers to work things out between them.

Andy's wanting to go out and not taking 'No' for an answer.

Mrs. B. told Andy that she had realised he could take care of himself, and that from now on he was to make the decisions about where he could go.

A few hours after she told him this, Andy tried her out, saying provocatively, 'Hey, Mum, I'm going to the bike shop.' Before, she might automatically have said, 'No, you can't.' This time she said simply, 'Well, that's your decision.' Andy seemed startled at getting this answer. A minute later he poked his head in the door and again told her, 'Mum, I *said*, I'm going to the bike shop!' Mrs. B. said, 'Mm hm.' Andy apparently still couldn't believe her, and said angrily, 'Mum, didn't you hear what I said? *I'm going to the bike shop!*' Mrs. B. said casually, 'Well, I'll see you later then.'

Andy never did go to the bike shop, but apparently he really thought about his mother's new stand. For several more weeks he continued to ask her permission to go places in this way, although by the end of that time he had the answer down pat, and he would say, 'Hey, Mum, can I go to John's house? . . . I know, I know, that's my decision.'

Staying up late.

The B.'s told both boys that they were old enough to supervise their own bedtime, and from then on said nothing about it at all.

Mr. and Mrs. B. also began focussing much more of their attention on things *they* wanted to do, and much less on Andy. In the first week, they went out for dinner by themselves twice, leaving both boys at home. Andy angrily accused them of never taking him anywhere, and Mr. B. told him he'd be glad to go out with him as soon as he felt sure he wouldn't be embarrassed by Andy's behaviour, and not before. The father was fully prepared, the next time Andy made a scene in a restaurant, to walk out and leave him sitting there. Apparently being ready to do so was enough, for he never actually had to do it.

In a week or so, when they were comfortable about having dropped their controls over kid's-life items, Mr. and Mrs. B. began working on parent's-life items.

Mrs. B. picked the morning breakfast mess to work on first. The first time she saw Andy after he'd left this mess was when he came home from school. For several days, then, as soon as she saw him in the afternoon, she said, 'Andy, will you please clean up the kitchen?' Andy responded with jokes, refusals, accusations ('You don't care about me') and so on, and Mrs. B. followed through with three or four repetitions of her three-part assertive sentence.

Mr. T. chose the problem of Andy's taking his tools. He was all ready to tell Andy that he wanted to feel secure about them, but the problem did not come up again!

The main result of the B.'s work seemed to be this: that Andy liked *being made responsible for himself, and when he was given this responsibility he stopped acting up.*

Within two months after they began working on their problems with Andy, the B.'s reported that there were no longer any real problems. As they put it, Andy had 'mellowed'. Both reported feeling closer to him than they ever had. When asked what had happened with the items on their lists, they reported on the ones they could still remember:

School. Andy was going to school regularly. He had got several black marks for forgetting his homework, and there had been one note from a teacher to Mrs. B. She gave this note to Andy, who told her he knew what it was about, that he knew it was his job to take care of it, and that he intended to do so!

Asked about the problem of Andy's not getting up in time for school, Mrs. B. said, 'Great'.

Yelling at his mother. This had stopped early on. Mr. B. had actually had to leave the room once, when his wife and Andy had an argument. He had a chance to say, 'I'm uncomfortable in this situation, and I'm going to leave the room', and do it. Only one other angry incident had occurred in this period: Andy told his folks he had left his bike at school and was going back to get it. Mrs. B. knew the school would be closed and, in a momentary throwback to previous habits, told him he couldn't go. In the old days, said the parents, a real scene would have ensued. This time, instead, Andy simply said huffily, 'This is my business!', picked up his coat, and walked out the door to go to the school. His mother thought it over and decided he was right.

Cleaning his room. This was no longer a problem. Dennis was now in charge of cleaning the whole room, as part of a deal the two boys had worked out.

Mess. Andy still sometimes left mess around the house. His father said, 'When he does that, I tell him "I'd like that mess cleaned up."

Occasionally he still needs to be reminded, and as long as I tell him, "*I* didn't leave a mess when I took a bath." he goes back and cleans it up.'

Staying up late. This was no longer a problem. The first few nights in which the parents said nothing about bedtime, both boys stayed up nearly all night. Said Mr. B., 'That must have worn them out. Starting with the third night, they went to bed at a very good time and even turned the lights out.'

Spitting had disappeared. 'We never mentioned that to him, and I have never seen him do it since.'

Stealing from the parents' room had stopped. 'We just told him our room was out of bounds.'

Demanding to be taken places didn't happen any more. One morning Andy *asked* his father courteously to take him to a football game that night, and Mr. B. felt good about doing so.

Wanting to leave the house. Andy was still 'independent' about this. If his mother objected to his going out, he would say something like, 'I want to, and if I get in trouble, it will be my own fault' – and go.

Not feeding the dogs. Andy still did not feed the dogs; he told his parents he didn't have time to do it before school, and suggested Dennis do it instead. He volunteered to do the outdoor jobs instead!

Molesting the dogs and cat. This hadn't happened in weeks.

Changing TV channels when parents are watching. Andy no longer did this. However, after he stopped doing it, Dennis tried it a few times. His mother told him, 'This new system isn't just for Andy. It applies to you, too.'

Embarrassing the parents in front of visitors. This item had actually reversed itself. Andy's grandfather had visited the family for several weeks, and instead of the harrowing times Andy had always given the family before when this happened, Mrs. B. reported that this time, 'He was so good with my father. He cried when his granddad left.'

An extra side-effect: The parents had forgotten to list nail-biting as a longterm problem. Without a word being said about it, it had disappeared during this period.

In fact, two months after beginning their work, the parents were no longer concerned about Andy's behaviour, and were beginning, instead, to use the skills they had learned with Andy to deal with various friends and relatives who, it seemed, had been taking advantage of them. For example, Mrs. B.'s brother regularly borrowed Mr. B.'s car, sometimes without asking, and yet refused to lend Mr. B. his motorbike, even though that sometimes left the B.'s without transport. Another relative had come to visit them and had now camped out for many weeks in their workshop, where he entertained his girl friends to the accompaniment of drink, loud music, and much worry for the B.'s about the example he was setting for their sons. It was hard for the B.'s even to say anything to these people, but when they finally did, they were surprised to find that these relationships improved because of it. All of this reaffirmed their new, solid way of dealing with Andy.

It seemed almost too good to be true that Andy should have changed so much because of what the parents had done, and Mr. and Mrs. B. could hardly believe it. They were halfway inclined to attribute the improvement to the fact that Andy had met some new friends and, especially, a very nice girl in his class. We agreed that the new girl friend was a real plus in the situation, but also told the parents we believed the bulk of the credit should go to them and the loving changes they had made.

Children Are Unique

A great deal of the way a young person develops seems to be determined by something inside the child. We think the way things went for Mrs. H. and her two children illustrates this.

Mrs. H. is a very easy going, soft hearted, and 'mellow' person, and if she had two children like her son Tom (10) she would probably never have had any problem. Tom was very much like her. However, Tim (12) was very much like her ex-husband – a very self-determined and self-sufficient, rugged, outdoors type of person. Tim loved to play, alone or with a friend, at a nearby stream where he would build shelters of branches, catch mice and frogs, and wade along the stream. Mrs. H. worried not only about all that activity but even that he had to cross a busy street at a zebra-crossing to get to the stream. He thought her concern was silly and simply did what he wanted to. He also pushed her in all sorts of ways, for example to give him money or buy things he wanted, and she was putty in his hands. He knew that if he made enough of a scene he would get what he wanted, and he was a champion scene-maker.

Mrs. H. was simply not able to take care of herself to the extent needed with Tim. She did make some changes of the sort we coached her to do and found that they were helpful. She also recognized that other things she simply couldn't do would have been beneficial as well. Tim was just too much for her, and she decided to see whether any of her family would be willing to have him. Her sister and brother-in-law – he is a commercial fisherman – really took to Tim, and they were eager to have him. Tim is now living with his uncle and aunt, and it is working out very well. Tim fishes with his uncle during the summers and appears to thrive on it. Mrs. H. and Tom are quite comfortable together.

A Second Marriage That Worked

For Mr. and Mrs. M. the principal item on their parent's-life lists was preserving their own relationship together against behaviour by their children and step-children which was driving them apart. Mr. and Mrs. M. had been married about a year when we first met them. They both brought children from previous marriages into the relationship. Mrs. M. had two girls aged 5 and 13, and Mr. M. had a daughter of 12. When they first came for help the problem, which had started with the two older girls, had become so serious that the parents themselves were close to breaking up. On the face of it, the things that brought the parents to this spot were not serious at all. The two girls would do things like leaving a mess in the kitchen or living room, or not putting their bicycles away. The difficulty was that the two parents would treat the two girls differently. Mrs. M. complained that her husband was too harsh a disciplinarian, especially with her daughter, and that he let his own 'angel' get away with a lot. Mr. M. said that basic discipline of the girls was his wife's job and she wasn't doing it, so he had to. He resented this, especially as it was her daughter, he said, who caused all the trouble. Mrs. M. was equally emphatic that *his* daughter was the real souce of their agony. (We believe they were both right. Children – and people in general – can be angels or devils selectively depending on the audience.)

The girls seemed to play parts well calculated to drive the parents apart. Mr. M.'s daughter did most of the things which particularly annoyed his wife, and his step-daughter knew precisely how to irritate him. The incident that brought the situation to a head was triggered by Mrs. M.'s daughter's bike. Mr. M. worked a late shift, and when he came home at midnight he liked to leave his garage door open and drive straight in. One night for the umpteenth time, he found his step-daughter's bike blocking his way. At this point he created a scene which soon involved the whole family.

We persuaded the M.'s to try an approach in which they would focus on taking care of their own relationship: in effect, to stand shoulder to shoulder rather than nose to nose. The two of them were to come up with a uniform method of discipline *if they could*, but if they couldn't, then each was to use his or her own preferred method.* Each girl was to be dealt with by the parent who first noticed any problem, and neither parent was to listen to private tales from a daughter about how evil her step-parent was. The parents also decided to begin referring to each girl as 'my daughter' and also to ask that they be called Dad or Mum by their step-daughters rather than by first names.

The M.'s were well motivated to save their marriage because it was basically a good one. Consequently they were able to begin changing the way they were with their daughters. For example, Mrs. M. would announce to both girls, 'I want the playroom kept clean of dirty dishes', and after the usual early responses parents get with that approach ('I didn't do it!', 'I didn't either.') she succeeded to a large extent in having the place cleaner. An important side effect was that she learned that she didn't really care as much as she thought she did that it had to be perfectly neat.

The father announced to both girls that if he saw any bicycle blocking his car, he would pay no attention to whose it was, but would wake both girls to come and put it away. And he did. As you might imagine, the bicycles very soon stopped blocking his path at night.

Mr. and Mrs. M. have now been married for an additional five years, and the two older girls are pretty well grown up. Very early, the girls gave up their provocative behaviour and each parent began experiencing loving feelings towards both girls. The favouritism disappeared. The parents are quite happy together, and they're both happy with all three girls. The girls have long since given up the behaviour that was dividing the parents and seem to be quite comfortable in the family.

A Second Marriage That Didn't Work

Not all 'second marriage' families are as successful as the M.'s.

---

*In all of our work, we emphasize that it is not necessary for parents to adopt a uniform attitude in dealing with the children, as long as there is not deliberate sabotage. For example, the bicycles were Mr. M.'s problem. If having them left in the middle of the garage floor didn't bother Mrs. M. she could simply do nothing about them and let it be a problem the girls would have with Mr. M. Of course, she should refrain from encouraging the girls to be careless about the bikes, directly or indirectly — that's sabotage — but simply not get involved one way or the other.

The L. family did not work out.

Mr. and Mrs. L. each brought a 14-year-old son into their marriage. One of them, Mr. L.'s son, was particularly active in what seemed like an attempt to cause problems between the parents. He was extremely surly with his step-mother, and in private talks with us he made it very clear that he wanted his original mother and his father to get together again, even though he knew it was very unlikely. He also said that even if his step-mother treated him as well as she treated his stepbrother (which he felt was excellent treatment), he would still not be nice to her.

Despite the fact that each of the parents recognized that the behaviour of the boys, particularly the father's boy, was driving a wedge between them, they have not been able to change the way they deal with them – to turn responsibilities for their own actions over to the boys and to stand together as a team to deal with the very important parent's-life item of damage to their relationship. In this instance, the only really major problem was the surliness of one of the boys in the presence of his step-mother. However, the parents were not able to revise the way they do things, and they are, at the time of writing, on the verge of separating.

A Long-Term Effort

Mrs. Z. had a strongly-engrained habit of ignoring her own wants and concentrating most of her energy on controlling her son's life, instead. Her story demonstrates how even a deeply engrained habit like this can be changed with time and an improved way of living result.

Mrs. Z., a computer programmer, had brought up her 14-year-old son Ted by herself, almost from his infancy. His father was long gone and nobody knew anything of his whereabouts. Mrs. Z. also had a crippled leg which meant that, except for short distances, she had to walk using crutches. She spent much of her energy worrying about whether Ted was doing 'right', and her imagination was most vivid. She originally phoned about guidance for Ted because she was suspicious that he was going to get an 11-year-old girl, who lived in a neighbouring flat, pregnant. She had no real evidence for her belief that there was sexual activity going on and when we looked into the matter, it seemed highly unlikely. Yet she worried, worried, worried, about what would happen if this pregnancy occurred – would she be responsible; what would happen to Ted; what would the other mother do to her, and so forth. She could imagine everyone in town reading about the situation in the newspaper, Ted's being named as the father, his having to marry the little girl and never finishing school, having to live all his life as a labourer, and so on. Other problems that bothered her had to do with the way the two of them lived together and Ted's not doing his fair share of the work. Because of her leg she could not carry out the rubbish and she had difficulty cleaning the bath. Those and some cleaning up chores were established as Ted's jobs, but he always shirked them.

Ted struck us as a basically solid boy, with a minor tendency to get into some mischief but generally doing well in school and getting an occasional lawn-mowing job on his own initiative. His main problem was that his mother was so tightly controlling him that he had very little feeling of running his own life. Even when he would get his lawn-mowing jobs, his mother would pressure him to make sure he did them exactly as she thought was right, that his customers were completely satisfied, and so on. She worried that they wouldn't be.

Mrs. Z. had had to make many personal sacrifices in order to raise Ted to adolescence, and in the process she had become almost entirely focussed on his life and welfare and had nearly forgotten what her own wants might be. In our work with her, we coached her on the very difficult task of dropping controls over Ted's life and picking up instead the responsibility for making her own life happy.

Mrs. Z. and we worked together for a long time. Over a period of approximately two years she very gradually changed, and little by little was able to let Ted run more of his own life. Each new item that came up was a struggle for her. He wanted to get a job. He wanted to go camping with an older boy who she acknowledged was a competent and experienced camper and whom she liked. He wanted to take a girl to the cinema. He wanted to enter a science exam. Each instance caused her to worry, and she was brilliant at imagining all sorts of exotic catastrophes that might ensue. However, she coped with each item as it arose and by the end of the two year period could look back with a bit of amusement at her earlier self. She was able to smile at the memory of her worry about Ted's getting the little girl pregnant, and to feel satisfied that yes, indeed, he was growing up to be quite a nice boy – even though he was doing things on his own and she had essentially given up control of his-life items.

During this period, she also began taking much better care of her own life. She learned that she loved going on weekend outings with two women friends, and began doing so. She enjoyed going to plays and concerts, and bought pairs of season tickets. If Ted wanted to go, which he often did, she invited him. If not, she found someone else to go with her. She engineered a modest shift in her work situation which gave her much greater satisfaction in her job. She realized she hated their flat, and moved to a nicer one, telling Ted she would be looking for some extra help in paying for it. Ted, too, wanted to live in a better flat, and enthusiastically agreed to this.

Ted is now approaching 17, at sixth-form college, and has held down an evening job for the past year in a cafe where he is now a manager. Sometimes he doesn't take the rubbish out spontaneously, but one reminder is usually all it takes. The bath-cleaning problem has disappeared because their new flat has a shower, which they both prefer anyway, and he washes the shower out to her satisfaction, using his flannel and his foot. They are quite happy together, and they both enjoy going to dinner and a concert together. He has developed a set of friends where they now live and she is quite content with them. Mrs. Z. took approximately two years to truly decide that yes, it was good for the two of them that she run her life and that she let him run his, and she is now reaping the harvest of that decision.

Getting Help

There is help available for the many different kinds of problems which parents face with their teenagers. A good starting point is to talk about the problem to one of the free telephone advisory services (see below), a teacher who may offer new insight into your teenager, or a school psychologist/counsellor. Advice is also available through your GP who may help directly or refer your teenager for specialist help (eg to a Child Guidance Clinic or a psychotherapist).

*If you want information about the various organisations who offer help visit your local **Citizens' Advice Bureau**. In some regions there are **Neighbourhood Advice Centres** which are similar to Citizens' Advice Bureaux. Look under 'Advice Centres' in the phone book or contact **The Federation of Independent Advice** on 01-274 1839.*

*If you want to talk to someone who specialises in teenage problems there are several organisations which will be able to help. Youth counselling services provide both information and befriending to young people and parents alike. For details about your nearest centre contact the **National Association of Young People's Counselling and Advisory Services**,17-23 Albion Street, Leicester LE1 6GD. Telephone Leicester (0533) 554775. **OPUS Organisations for Parents Under Stress**, c/o Natalie Long, 26 Manor Drive, Pichering, North Yorkshire YO18 8DD is an umbrella body for groups such as Parents Anonymous and Parents Helpline which provide a friendly telephone advisory service. The **Samaritans** offer 24-hour help to anyone, but especially to people with emotional problems and to those who are feeling* 'suicidal or despairing'. Look under 'Samaritans' in the phone book. Sometimes what seems to be a problem with a teenager involves the whole family. Helpful organisations include the **Marriage Guidance Council** — look under Marriage Guidance Council in the local phone book. **The Association of Family Therapy**, Social Services Dept, Lewis House, Manvers Street, Bath BA1 1JG can tell you where you will find your nearest family therapy clinic.

Below is a list of a few organisations which offer help for particular problems:
Al-Anon, 61 Great Dover Street, London SE1. Tel: 01-403 0888 (alcoholic problems)
Release, 1 Elgin Avenue, London, W9. Tel: 01-289 1123 (a national advisory service on drug-related difficulties, including trouble with the law and the legal system.)
Institute For The Study Of Drug Dependence, Kingsbury House, 3 Blackburn Road, London NW6. Tel: 01-328 5541.
National Campaign Against Solvent Abuse, 55 Wood Street, Mitcham Junction, Surrey. Tel: 01-640 2946 (glue-sniffing)
Action on Smoking and Health, 5/11 Mortimer Street, London W1N 7RM. Tel: 01-637 9843 (ASH can tell you where you'll find your nearest group.)
Young Gamblers Anonymous. Look under Gamblers Anonymous in the phone book (offers help to young people who are addicted to fruit machines or gambling).
The Joint Council for Gay Teenagers (BM JCGT London WC1N 3XX)
Family Planning Clinics run by the NHS (for practical help about contraception and sexual problems).
Brook Advisory Centres (for advice about sexual matters).
British Pregnancy Advisory Service, Austy Manor, Wootton Wawen, Solihull, W. Midlands. Tel: 056 423225.
Education Welfare Office (contact your local authority listed in the phone book and ask for the Education Welfare section of the Education Department (for help on truancy and general matters about your teenager's welfare at school).

Index

About the Authors

Jean and Bob Bayard have been a team for thirty-six years. Both psychologists, they have a clinical practice together in California. They have raised five children together; when their youngest reached eighteen, they had had thirty-two consecutive years of bringing up children. By that time they had experienced at first hand most of the problems they discuss in this book.

Jean is a psychotherapist and specializes in helping women fulfil their full potential. She is a writer, a serious student of philosophy and she supports Greenpeace and every sincere attempt to take care of human beings and their world.

Bob's first career was as a physicist and manager of technical research and development. It included a year spent as a United Nations Technical Assistance Expert in Thailand. In 1975, at the age of fifty-five, he took his second Ph.D. in psychology, and has been working as a psychotherapist ever since. He specializes in problems of families and of couples.

Other gift books from Exley Publications

Choices: a teenage girl's practical workbook for career and personal planning, £6.95. A book that every mother, grandmother, aunt and mentor will want to give 'to the teenage' women in their lives. It's beautiful, but eminently teaches young girls to be independent and self-reliant.

Sharing Nature with Children, £3.50. This book contains over forty games which children can play in the country, in city parks, and in their own gardens. The games are fun, but they also bring a real understanding of nature, camouflage, the roles of hunter and hunted, and the natural balance of living things.

Free Stuff for Kids, £4.50. This book will bring a lot of fun to children aged six to thirteen. There are so many things to write for from the Post Office, Nestlé, PG Tips, Kodak, Longleat Stanley Gibbons and dozens upon dozens of other firms. And they're all either free or up to £1. The book is educational too — it teaches children to write and receive letters, and gets them involved in creative hobbies. A very special present, full of potential activity.

Feeding your Child, £4.95. Sound, practical advice on the correct feeding of babies and young children, as well as pregnant mums. The author is a nutritionist and a mother. A useful book for parents and health visitors.

Is there Life after Housework? £5.95. a revolutionary book which sets out to show how you can save up to 75% of the time you now spend on cleaning. It is written by a man who heads one of the largest cleaning firms in the world. Humorous illustrations throughout. It's a natural gift to the hardpressed and downtrodden!

Grandmas and Grandpas, £3.95. Children are close to grandparents, and this book of children sayings, written entirely by children reflects that warmth: 'Your granny loves you, no matter what you do'; 'A grandma is old on the outside but young on the inside'. 'A granny is jolly and when she laughs a warmness spreads over you.' This is a very, very popular book, which makes a particularly loving present for grandparents.

Love, a celebration, £4.95. Writers and poets old and new have captured the feeling of being in love in this very personal collection. Some of the best love messages of all ages are sensitively illustrated with fine photograms and grey screened photographs. And to enhance the collection the book is bound in a rich wine-red suedel cloth and finished with gold tooling, gift wrapped and sealed with wax. This is our best-selling book — it makes an ideal love-gift.

Marriage, a keepsake, £4.95. In the same series, but with a dove-grey suedel cover. This collection of poems and prose celebrates marriage with some of the finest love messages between husbands and wives. A gift for all ages — from those about to be married to those who *have known fifty good years and more together. Giftwrapped with sealing wax.*

Old is . . . great! *£3.25. A wicked book of cartoons which pokes fun at youth and revels in the first grey hairs of middle age. 'Extremely funny' (Daily Telegraph).*

Free colour catalogue available on request. Books may be ordered through your bookshop, or by post from Exley Publications, Dept. HT1, 16 Chalk Hill, Watford, Herts, United Kingdom WD1 4BN. Please add 50p per book for postage and packing.

Exley Publications reserves the right to show new retail prices on books, which may differ from those previously advertised.